DYNAMIC AIKIDO

Dynamic
AIKIDO

By **GŌZŌ SHIODA**

translated by
GEOFFREY HAMILTON

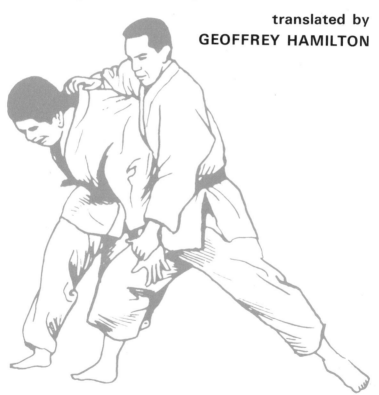

Published by
KODANSHA INTERNATIONAL LTD.
Tokyo, Japan & Palo Alto, Calif., U.S.A.

Distributed in the British Commonwealth (excluding Canada) by
Ward Lock & Company Limited., London and Melbourne; in Continental
Europe by Boxerbooks, Inc., Zurich; and in the Far East by Japan
Publications Trading Co., C.P.O. Box 722, Tokyo.

   Published by Kodansha International Ltd., 2-12-21, Otowa,
Bunkyo-ku, Tokyo, Japan and Kodansha International/USA, Ltd.,
577 College Avenue, Palo Alto, California 94306.

Contents

Photographs for Sections 1, 2 and 3 by Fumio Matsuda; photographs for Section 4 by Seiji Muto; and jacket photograph by Saburo Nagamatsu.

Preface

The object of this book is to provide an introduction to aikido which can be used as a text book by beginners. The techniques described have been selected from those used in everyday practice at the Tokyo Yōshinkan, and they include the essential basic movements.

Every effort has been made to present a simple classification of the techniques and to describe them in straightforward, easily understandable terms. However, as with all the Japanese martial arts, there are many points in aikido which cannot be adequately explained with words and photographs; so while this book can never satisfactorily replace a qualified teacher, it is hoped that it will provide a useful supplement to personal instruction.

I should like to express my appreciation to Seishi Terada, Takashi Kushida, Kyōichi Inoue, to all the instructors at the Yōshinkan who appear in the photographs as my opponents, and to those students who also gave their time and energy. I am also indebted to my seniors and the directors of the Yōshinkan for their help and advice in the planning of this book. Lastly, I should like to thank Geoffrey Hamilton for writing the English translation of this book and for compiling the section on practical application.

GŌZŌ SHIODA

Translator's Introduction

Since the original version of this book was intended to be read by Japanese, it presumed on the part of the reader a background knowledge of Japanese history and culture. Furthermore, there is certain terminology used in describing the Japanese martial arts which most Japanese understand or can guess at but which is meaningless when directly translated into English.

The following notes attempt to explain or amplify some of these points for the Western reader.

THE SAMURAI: Until just about one hundred years ago Japan was a feudal country. The land was broken down into fiefs and society into four immutable strata. At the bottom were the merchants, above them the craftsmen, then the farmers and at the top the military class, the samurai.

The samurai's allegiance was to his feudal lord. In return for his stipend he was expected to fight and, if necessary, die for that lord. After 1600 Japan was free from civil war and for the next two and half centuries the samurai as a class were mainly concerned with administration, but it was still their duty to practice the martial arts and it was during this period that these arts were refined and categorized. They also became means of inculcating self-discipline and philosophy, particularly that of Zen.

THE "WAYS": The original Japanese word for martial arts was *bujutsu*—the first character *"bu"* meaning "military", the second *"jutsu"* meaning "art". After Japan emerged from the feudal period in the 1860's the arts were studied less for the value of their practical application and more stress was laid on their philosophical elements. To indicate this shift of emphasis the second character *"jutsu"* was replaced with the character *"dō"* which has an abstract meaning of "way" in the Zen sense, which is a practice that can lead to enlightenment. Hence *kenjutsu* ("fencing") has become *kendō*, *kyūjutsu* ("archery") has become *kyūdō* etc.

AIKIDO : The fundamental principle in aikido is to be so "in tune" with the opponent that one can sense his intentions and be able to take advantage of his movement. This principle has given aikido its name: the character *"ai"* means "to meet", the character *"ki"* means "spirit" and *"dō"* means "the way" in the philosophical sense explained above.

AIKIDO AND THE SWORD: In explaining aikido techniques constant reference is made to the use of the sword. Needless to say, this refers to the Japanese sword which is generally held in two hands and carried directly in the front of the body, the hands level with the solar plexus and the shoulders and hips square to the opponent.

When a stroke is made in *kendō* (Japanese fencing) the movement originates from the hips. When the sword is raised (and this is the movement most often cited in aikido) it is as though the hips push in the direction of the elbows in an attempt to raise them. Both hands are brought level with or just above the forehead and in line with the center of the body.

ATEMI: These are blows delivered against certain vulnerable points of the body with the tips of the fingers, side of the hand, elbow, knee, toes, heels etc. The blow most often cited in this text is *metsubushi* ("smashing of the eyes") and is delivered by the knuckle at the base of the middle finger to the point directly between the eyes.

"SECURE" AND "CONTROL": The word "secure" is used in this context to indicate the moment when a lock becomes effective, i.e., begins to cause pain. "Control" is used to indicate what is often the final stage of a movement when the opponent is completely immobilized or at least unable to make any effective movement.

"OPENING" THE BODY: This is a convenient way of describing the action of pivoting on one foot or the other and taking back one side of the body in one piece, e. g., like opening a door.

"FLOATING": This refers in the intransitive to the moment when a person's weight is rising as the result of natural movement, e.g., walking. In the transitive it means reinforcing the opponent's upward movement. It does not have the sense of lifting.

G. H.

History of Aikido

Since the end of the war, and particularly during the last decade, the ancient Japanese martial art of aikido has enjoyed a rapidly expanding popularity, not only in the country of its origin but also abroad, especially in America, Europe, and Southeast Asia.

Originally, the martial arts were simply methods of defense and attack used in serious combat that consisted of primitive hand-to-hand and stick fighting techniques. At times a small and comparatively weak man would overcome a bigger opponent; and when the reason for his victory was appreciated a new method would be formulated. Thus, over the years, teachers and practitioners of the arts—sometimes at considerable risk to themselves—have refined and developed these techniques which today stand up to scientific scrutiny.

However, as the martial arts became influenced by Buddhist concepts they were transformed from mere collections of techniques to philosophical "ways". Their dimensions grew until they went beyond the simple objective of killing the enemy to embrace many elements concerned with day to day living. In other words they changed from ways of killing to ways of life. Particularly after the demise of the samurai class, the martial "arts" became martial "ways," and great value was placed upon them as a means of generating the moral strength necessary to build a sound society. Nevertheless, in the last analysis the martial arts are the arts of the fighting men—of the samurai—and if the basic objective of defeating the enemy is lost sight of, then as martial arts they must cease to exist. Accordingly, they must not become mere intellectual exercises, the fundamental *budō* "conduct" must not be treated lightly and the "way of technique" must not be neglected as a form of spiritual and physical training.

There are still insufficient data available concerning the history of aikido, and while no doubt more will be discovered the following is an outline of what has been learned so far.

Present day aikido has its origin in *daitō aikijutsu* which is

Shinra Saburō
Yoshimitsu

Morihei Ueshiba

said to have been founded by Prince Teijun, the sixth son of the Emperor Seiwa (850-880 A. D.). Through the prince's son, Tsunemoto, it was passed on to succeeding generations of the Minamoto family. By the time the art had reached Shinra Saburō Yoshimitsu, the younger brother of Yoshiie Minamoto, it would appear that the foundations of the present aikido had already been laid. Yoshimitsu was apparently a man of exceptional skill and learning and it is said that he devised much of his technique after watching a spider skillfully trap a large insect in its fine web. It is recorded that Yoshimitsu studied anatomy by dissecting the bodies of war dead and criminals; and his house, "Daitō Mansion" has given its name to his system of aikijutsu.

Yoshimitsu's second son, Yoshikiyo, lived in Takeda, in the province of Kai, and he eventually became known by this name. Subsequently the techniques were passed on to successive generations as the secret art of the Takeda house and made known only to members and retainers of the family. In 1574, Takeda Kunitsugu moved to Aizu and the techniques passed on to his descendants came to be known as the Aizu-todome techniques.

Thereafter the art remained an exclusively samurai practice and was handed down within the family until Japan emerged from isolation into the Meiji period in 1868. At that time Sōkaku Takeda Sensei, then head of the family, began to teach the art outside the Takeda household, traveling widely throughout Japan and finally settling in Hokkaidō. His son, Tokimune Takeda Sensei, opened the Daitōkan dōjō in Abashiri, Hokkaidō, and continues to further the development of aikido as the head of the Daitō school.

The most outstanding of Sōkaku Takeda's pupils was Morihei Ueshiba. Ueshiba Sensei, a man of rare ability, brought to the Daitō school the essentials of other ancient schools of the martial arts and added techniques of his own devising to found modern aikido. For many years Ueshiba Sensei has taught and guided from his dōjō in Wakamatsu-cho in Tokyo. He is now over eighty years old and is still very active. Ueshiba's dōjō, Aikido Honbu,

Sōkaku Takeda

Yōshinkan Dōjō

is now supervised by his son Kisshomaru Ueshiba, who has devoted himself to the dissemination of aikido throughout Japan and overseas with great success.

A distinguished pupil of Ueshiba Sensei, Kenji Tomiki of Waseda University, is very active in the field of physical education and had concentrated on developing aikido as a sport.

One of Ueshiba's most outstanding pupils has been Gōzō Shioda (9th dan), the author of this book and the director of the Aikido Yōshinkan, who has contributed much to bring about the popularity that aikido has enjoyed since the war. Shioda entered Ueshiba Sensei's dōjō at the age of eighteen and lived there for eight years and even as a student he displayed the clear-cut, graceful technique and extraordinary vigor we see today. Like Sōkaku Takeda and Morihei Ueshiba, Shioda Sensei is small, weighing only 108 pounds, and the fact that in spite of this he has become so formidable is, I feel, the rationale of aikido.

The tremendous interest shown in aikido since the war probably dates back to 1954 when, under the auspices of the Life Extension Society, an exhibition of Japanese martial arts was organized in Tokyo. Shioda Sensei took part and his demonstration attracted a great deal of attention and favorable comment. From then on, aikido gained popularity so rapidly that within a year a group of financiers established the Aikido Yōshinkan (President Shōshirō Kudō) and placed Shioda Sensei in charge.

When one considers that before the war aikido was practiced by just a few individuals and special army and navy groups, the present growth and popularity of the art is indeed gratifying. However this rapid expansion has created a demand for qualified teachers and the future development of aikido will be determined by the degree of success in producing persons capable of teaching and maintaining the high standards of the art.

Finally, I hope teachers whose names I have no space to mention will forgive me and accept my gratitude for their efforts.

HIROSHI TAKEUCHI

As with all the martial arts aikido owes its development to the countless teachers and practitioners who over the past eight hundred years have devised and polished the techniques, sometimes at the risk of their lives. These techniques are based on principles which today stand up to scientific scrutiny. One of the characteristic principles of aikido is *marui* ("circular motion"). If an attack launched along a straight line is "received" with a circular motion it can be channeled and controlled, and once this circular movement has been mastered it is possible to meet an attack of any force from any direction. Furthermore the concept of meeting something in a circular way is one which can be used in everyday situations. Progress can only be made in the study of technique by remaining calm and practicing in harmony with one's opponent. Real strength consisits of a straight but flexible mind and a body tempered by hard practice. (*Pictured right is kokyū nage.*)

SECTION 1

The Nature of Aikido

The Harmony of Aikido
and The Mind

A fundamental axiom of aikido is that the gentle can control the strong through the study of technique. However, aikido is more than simply a physical skill. To coordinate with the opponent's movement and power it is necessary that the mind as well as the body be pliant. In other words the mind must be alert and flexible in order to be able to take advantage of the opponent's movements. Taken a step further, this means that the *aikidoka* must understand his opponent and share his feelings; so the final objective is not to inflict injury but to cultivate a sense of harmony.

Thus contest, which leads to superiority and defeatist complexes, is avoided in practicing aikido, and the techniques are safely assimilated in kata form i.e., in cooperation with a partner each movement is repeated until it has been thoroughly absorbed and has become a reflex action. Aikido is not concerned merely with relationships between people; it is a form of training in which the *aikidoka* learns to harmonize with nature through the practice of natural techniques. A movement that is awkward or forced cannot be aikido.

Technique and Practice

ANALYSIS OF TECHNIQUE

Technique is the means of achieving maximum effect with the minimum of effort. Essentially this is done by using the force of one's opponent to his disadvantage. Thus, when pushed, the *aikidoka* moves with the direction of the attack, adding his own power to the force of his opponent. Similarly, if pulled, rather than pull in the opposite direction, he adds his own weight and movement to the pull, applies the appropriate technique and thereby brings the opponent under control. He wins, not as a result of a contest of strength, but by utilizing the force of his opponent.

Though most techniques center on the situation where two unarmed men are facing each other, there are techniques for various situations: armed man versus armed man, unarmed man versus armed man, one man against a number of opponents. As a result over three thousand techniques have been formulated of which some one hundred and fifty are basic techniques.

Repeated practice of these basic techniques opens the way to mastering the remainder.

CLASSIFICATION AND NOMENCLATURE OF TECHNIQUE

Aikido techniques are classified in the following way: *tachi waza* (both standing); *suwari waza* (both sitting); and *hanmi-hantachi waza* (one sitting and one standing). These groups are further divided into *nage waza* ("throwing techniques") and *osae waza* ("controlling techniques"). Most basic techniques incorporate *te waza* ("hand techniques"). This was because in ancient times armor was worn on the battlefield and the opponent's hands were accessible and vulnerable.

Since aikido embraces thousands of techniques, it is almost impossible to give them all a name; as a result only the basic techniques are identified and are referred to merely as *ikkajō, nikajō* (first, second classification) etc. This means that it is difficult for the ordinary person to ascertain the nature of the technique simply by hearing its name. For the beginner it is better to concentrate on learning the movement itself than to memorize the various names.

Old books on martial arts use abstruse explanations and learned nomenclature—this is thought to have been done deliberately to prevent the secrets of their art from being stolen. Again, it is probable that Zen priests from institutions and temples associated with the samurai families were called upon for help in recording techniques and methods which would account for the esoteric tone of the writings.

PRACTICE METHODS

Though aikido is normally practiced in kata form, this does not mean that the movement is "dead"; on the contrary, each repetition must be effective. The essence of aikido practice is that both partners perfect their movements and try to obtain real strength by applying the techniques correctly. Though aikido differs from other sports in that it goes beyond the normal concepts of victory and defeat, the object of controlling the opponent and gaining superiority must never be forgotten. At the same time, as mentioned earlier, the *aikidoka* must always strive for "mental harmony."

When performed correctly aikido technique requires no undue effort. Furthermore, no aikido technique requires abnormal physical power; anyone who can lift approximately sixteen pounds has sufficient strength—and if at any time a great deal of power is required to execute a technique, it is safe to conclude that the execution is bad. Thus, since aikido can be practiced as energetically or gently as desired, it can be enjoyed by people of all ages and both sexes. Moreover, aikido also promotes physical health, is a method of self-defense, means of cultivating the mind and, in the case of women, can be an aid to beauty since it improves deportment.

Circular Motion

The secret of being able to take advantage of the opponent's physical strength in aikido lies in the principle of *marui* ("circular") motion. Almost no movement in aikido follows a straight line: movement of feet, trunk and arms all describe an arc and, furthermore, are three-dimensional in that they follow the lines of a sphere or at times a spiral. Circular motion enables the *aikidoka* to add his weight and power to the opponent's pushing or pulling movement without fear of collision.

Changing direction illustrates the efficacy of circular movement. If the initial movement of the body is in a straight line it is necessary to pause to change direction; but if the initial movement is circular it is not necessary to interrupt the flow of movement. Pivoting of the body on either foot, moving along an arc and movement of the hands as though following the contours of a globe are frequently occurring examples of circular motion.

A prime concern when preparing this book was adequately to convey this circular movement. The student is urged to pay close attention to what is probably the most important basic movement in aikido by careful study of the photographs of the movements taken from above.

SPHERICAL MOVEMENT

Circular movement is not confined to one plane; it can range from front to rear, right to left, upward or downward, i.e., a competent *aikidoka* must be able to apply it in any direction along the surface of sphere if he wishes to negate an attack from any quarter.

CENTRIPETAL AND CENTRIFUGAL FORCE

Circular (or spherical) movement naturally embodies both centripetal and centrifugal force. The former is the force that draws things into a whirlpool or typhoon; the latter is the force that throws things off a spinning top. Analysis of a perfectly timed and executed technique shows that aikido makes use of these forces.

In the majority of cases where an opponent's balance has been completely broken, it has been by a spinning or turning movement rather than a direct attack. To consider this movement in more detail, suppose the opponent strikes directly from the front. Instead of meeting the attack head on, if one moves out of its path and, without opposing the opponent's movement, applies light upward pressure spirally, with very little effort it is possible to change the direction of the attack, destroy the opponent's balance and deprive him of his strength. This is analogous to the power of a tornado as compared with that of a wind blowing in a single direction.

The Essentials of Movement

SPEED

In aikido, as in most sports, speed is a vital element. Essentially there are two uses of speed: the first is to keep up with the opponent's movement, the second is to be able to avoid an initial attack. As an example of the first, it would be impossible to jump aboard a train moving at 120 mph but if one were aboard a vehicle traveling alongside the train in the same direction at the same speed this would be comparatively simple. As an example of the second use of speed, supposing a heavy object was falling directly overhead, one would move quickly to avoid being crushed. It is sufficient that one move just before the object strikes and just enough to avoid it.

Speed must not be gauged simply in relation to the opponent's capacity and certainly it is not sufficient to develop only enough to outstrip the average man—in aikido one must continually strive to build up exceptional speed.

TIMING

Timing is the synchronization of one's own movements with those of the opponent—this is the essence of aikido. This is in turn a combination of speed and concentration of energy (which is explained next). Timing might be described as the ability to judge the moment a wave begins to fall back after striking a rock.

In the photographs below the opponent leaps forward thrusting with both hands at my shoulders. At the right moment, the flow of force is reversed and the opponent is thrown. The vital part of the movement is the timing of the counter-thrust.

CONCENTRATION OF POWER

Shūchū-ryoku is the concentration of the whole of one's power at a given instant at a given point. For example, if one grasps one's opponent's wrist all one's strength should be directed at that point. Conversely, if one attempts *atemi* (explained in the Translator's Introduction) with one's right hand while part of one's strength is being used by the left, the blow will lose much of its effectiveness.

Though total concentration of strength is not possible, with regular training a remarkable level can be achieved. Even untrained people have been known in emergencies—such as a fire—to lift objects which would normally be too heavy for them; this is an example of unconscious concentration of strength. But with training it is possible to develop the ability to concentrate one's strength at will.

MOVING THE CENTER OF GRAVITY

By shifting the weight and by adjusting its distribution over each foot, the force of any technique can be doubled. In fact the degree of effectiveness of technique depends on the extent to which the weight is properly utilized. Great emphasis is placed on transferring the center of gravity in the basic movements of aikido and the student should keep this in mind constantly during practice.

However solid a building may appear, it is worthless if its foundations have not been well laid. This is also true of the body; however well developed the upper torso may be, if the legs and hips are weak it is impossible to apply or generate any real strength. Conversely, a man with relatively weak arms is difficult to defeat if his legs and hips are above average strength.

Firm foundations are essential in aikido, for without them it is impossible to develop effective technique. Basic posture and basic movement are the foundations of aikido, and, even after some progress has been made in the study of technique, they should be repeatedly practiced as part of daily routine. The fundamental movements and postures which are detailed in this section are an integral part of the basic techniques of Section 3. By perfecting all postures, movements and techniques, the *aikidoka* builds up a repertoire of skills which becomes a permanent part of himself.

SECTION 2
Posture & Movement

1 Kamae
"Posture" (when practiced alone)

Two basic postures are used in aikido: *migi-hanmi* ("right posture") and *hidari-hanmi* ("left posture"). It is essential that they be studied thoroughly because not only do all aikido techniques originate from them, but also, once mastered, they induce the correct mental attitude.

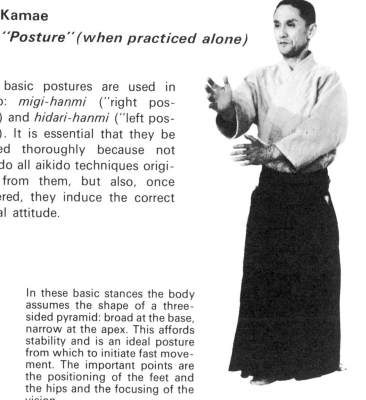

In these basic stances the body assumes the shape of a three-sided pyramid: broad at the base, narrow at the apex. This affords stability and is an ideal posture from which to initiate fast movement. The important points are the positioning of the feet and the hips and the focusing of the vision.

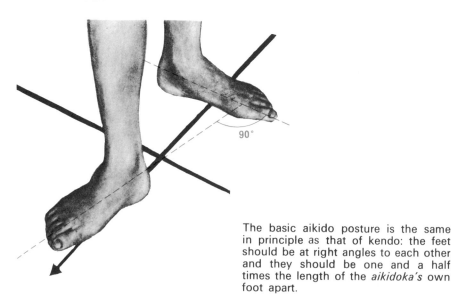

90°

The basic aikido posture is the same in principle as that of kendo: the feet should be at right angles to each other and they should be one and a half times the length of the *aikidoka's* own foot apart.

MIGI-HANMI ("*right posture*")

To ensure maximum stability and allow rapid movement forward and backward, keep the feet one and a half times the length of one's own foot apart and keep about two-thirds of the weight on the leading foot. The right arm should be held at chest level with the elbow slightly bent; the left hand should be held about four inches in front of the abdomen; and both hands should be in line with the center of the body. The fingers should be spread and pointed forward. The eyes should be centered—not focused—on a spot between the opponent's eyes so as to take in his whole body without concentrating the vision on any particular portion.

2 Kamae
"Posture" (when practiced with opponent)

There are two terms for describing the relative postures adopted when two *aikidoka* are practicing:

AI-HANMI (opposite page, top)

This is the situation in which the opponents are in the same posture i.e., both right or both left.

GYAKU-HANMI (opposite page, bottom)

This is the situation when the opponents use different postures, i.e., one right and the other left.

● *MAAI*

Maai is the appropriate distance (for both attack and defense) maintained between the opponents. If that distance is reduced, it becomes easier to attack and more difficult to defend; if the distance is increased the reverse is true. It is necessary to adopt the appropriate *maai* in each circumstance and in aikido practice it is normal to maintain a distance of roughly six feet.

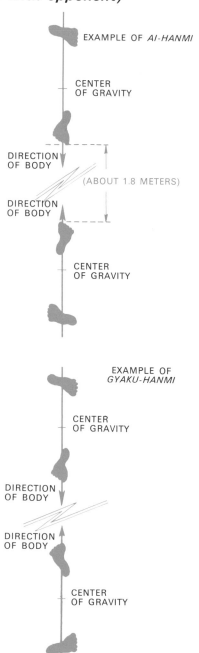

EXAMPLE OF *AI-HANMI*

CENTER OF GRAVITY

DIRECTION OF BODY

(ABOUT 1.8 METERS)

DIRECTION OF BODY

CENTER OF GRAVITY

EXAMPLE OF *GYAKU-HANMI*

CENTER OF GRAVITY

DIRECTION OF BODY

DIRECTION OF BODY

CENTER OF GRAVITY

AI-HANMI

GYAKU-HANMI

IMPORTANT POINTS ABOUT KAMAE

● Spread the fingers; keep the back and hips straight.
● Focus on the opponent's eyes, but keep his whole body in view; concentrate the attention in front, but do not let the head come forward.
● Keep the hips flexible and try to feel the power flowing from the feet to the fingertips.

3 Changing Position
(when pushed)

Kihon dōsa is the fundamental movement used to move out of the line of the opponent's attack by pivoting on either foot to assume a safe position from which the opponent can be controlled.

● The degree of the turn can vary though usually it is 95°.

◀ *Tori* is in *migi-gyaku-hanmi*. *Uke* attacks by grasping *tori's* right hand with his left and pushing.

1

● Throughout the whole movement *suri-ashi* should be used, i.e., rather than lift the feet, slide them without losing contact with the ground. In this way the weight will not "float."

▶ Placing all his weight on the right foot and pivoting on it *tori* brings his left foot round to the rear, describing an arc and maintaining contact with the ground. At the same time, without bending the elbow, he describes a small circle with the right hand, bringing the palm upward and, with a thrusting action, allows the momentum of *uke's* attack to continue forward.

2

● The right hand is turned palm upward, the elbow almost straightened, the left foot brought 95° to the rear and *uke's* forward movement reinforced.

● The weight is brought over the right knee, the leg almost straight and firmly braced.

▲ The distance between the feet is slightly wider than in *hanmi*. The nips are lowered and the upper and lower parts of the body assume the form of a cross to give a stable posture from which the movement can be initiated rapidly.

● The right hand is brought up to chest level, the feet are in line, the left hand is in front of the abdomen and parallel with the right hand.

◄ *Tori's* strength is flowing in the direction of his finger tips and his vision is concentrated beyond them.

4　Changing Position
(when pulled)

This is a basic movement to counter the opponent's force when being pulled, by moving forward while maintaining a strong, stable posture.

The movement is called *irimi* and is a basic technique peculiar to aikido.

▲ *Tori* and *uke* face each other in *migi-hanmi*. *Uke* grasps *tori's* right hand with his left and pulls strongly.

● *Tori's* right hand, palm upward, rises diagonally from the left side of *uke's* chest to his right shoulder, the thrust following the line of *tori's* feet.

▶ With a slight curving movement *tori* slides his right foot forward without lifting it from the ground (*suri-ashi*) to a spot inside and a third of a pace beyond *uke's* left foot. At the same time *tori's* hands move forward in unison with the right leg.

● The left hand moves forward horizontally to the center of *uke's* chest as if to deliver a blow (*atemi*) with the edge of the hand.

● The eyes look behind the finger tips of the right hand.

◀ The right hand, palm upwards, thrusts across *uke's* chest and over his right shoulder. When making this movement, *tori* should feel he is thrusting with a sword. As the right leg moves in, the hips follow to bring the center of gravity forward, the thrust originating from the left foot.

Once the body has moved forward, using *suri-ashi* the left foot closes up to its normal distance from the right foot.

● The feet form the letter "T".

5 Developing Hiriki
"Elbow power" (forward movement)

This is a basic movement designed to develop the correct use of the elbows and to train the hands, feet and body to move along a single line. Moreover, by practicing this movement *kokyū-ryoku* (*see* Page 120) can be acquired. *Kokyū-ryoku,* which becomes indispensable when the study of the techniques begins, embraces more than mere strength: it is a consolidation of all the individual's powers including breathing, willpower and mental vigor.

▲ *Tori* assumes right *gyaku-hanmi*. *Uke* grasps *tori's* right wrist with both hands.

▲ *Tori* advances using *suri-ashi*, moving one foot and almost simultaneously bringing up the other to restore the standard distance between the feet. The fingers are spread and the thrust flows to the hands from the feet, through the hips, chest, shoulders, elbows and wrists.

● The feet are prone to "float" during this movement which will result in the balance becoming unstable.

4

3

▲ Both hands push strongly forward and upward as though raising a sword.

▲ The right hand is above the left, the elbows slightly splayed, the shoulders down and the eyes and attention focused ahead.

6 Developing Hiriki
"Elbow power" (retiring movement)

This movement develops the ability to: 1) maintain a stable posture by changing the position of the weight, and 2) concentrate movement along a single line. It also develops strong but supple legs and hips and, like the former exercise, generates *kokyū-ryoku*.

◆ The fingers are spread; the arms extended with the elbows slightly bent; and the shoulders lowered. In this posture there should be a feeling that the power is flowing downward through the fingers of the right hand.

◆ Pivoting on the toes of both feet, *tori* turns 180°, transferring the weight from the left to the right leg.

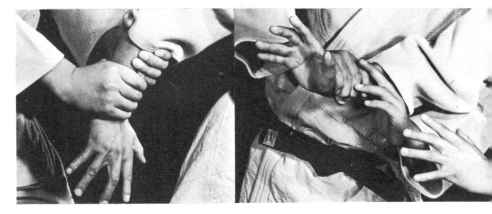

3

4

♦ As *tori* turns his body he also turns his right arm and raises both hands.

♦ When the movement is complete *tori's* left leg, hips and trunk are in line and the center of gravity is further over the right leg than in the previous exercise (*hiriki*—forward movement).

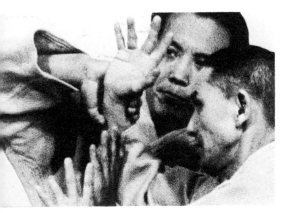

● The right arm is straightened as far as possible.
● The hips must not be lowered.
● Vertical movement of the body must be kept to the minimum, and when pivoting on the toes the heels must not be raised.

7 Shūmatsu Dōsa

"Fixing movement" (when pulled)

This movement embodies the basic "cutting with a sword" motion: the raising of the *tegatana* ("hand-sword") and the downward cutting stroke. Practice of the movement is good training for stability, *maai*, weight shifting and the mental aspects of aikido. *Shihō-nage* (*see* Page 48) is the basis of this technique.

● This movement is directly connected with the first *shihō-nage* of Section 3.

▶ In right *ai-hanmi, uke* grasps *tori's* wrists from the front.

▲ While sliding forward with the right foot (*suri-ashi*) *tori* lowers his body and thrusts his hands forward as though stabbing with a sword.

▶ Next *tori* takes a big step with his left foot (*suri-ashi*) and raising both hands (still being held by *uke*) above his head, throws his weight forward onto his left foot.

5

● During the whole of the movement *uke's* hands are directly in front of *tori*.

▶ *Tori* slides his right foot forward (*suri-ashi*) and extending his arms, brings them sharply down in a cutting motion to shoulder level. His weight is now well forward and his posture stable.

● *Uke* attempts to push *tori's* head forward.

4

◀ Pivoting on the toes of both feet, with a fast, twisting movement *tori* turns 180° and raises both hands high above his head. His weight is now on his right foot.

8 Shūmatsu Dōsa
"Fixing movement"

In the previous *shūmatsu dōsa* movement the motion was forward. In this movement the turn is made to the rear. Both movements are the same in principle.

◀ *Tori* is in left *gyaku-hanmi*, when *uke* grasps both wrists from the front and pushes.

● When turning, the toes of the foot describe a big arc.

● This is an example of *tori* skillfully using *uke's* power.

▲ *Tori* raises his right arm—the elbow down and the back of the hand upward—above his head, lifting *uke's* left arm. *Tori's* left hand is also raised but moves with the palm upward in a scooping movement.

5

● *Uke* takes a pace sideways with the left foot into the same position he is in at the end of the previous *shūmatsu dōsa* movement.

▶ *Tori* slides the right foot forward (*suri-ashi*) and the left foot follows without the heel being raised. Straightening his arms *tori* brings both hands down to shoulder level with a strong cutting motion.

4

3

● The fingers must be extended throughout the movement.
● *Tori* must synchronize his movement with that of *uke*.

● As a rule, when the left foot moves forward, the heel should not be raised.

▲ *Tori* again turns 180° and, still grasped by *uke*, the arms are raised higher above the head.

POSTURE & MOVEMENT **39**

9 Shikkō
"Moving on the knees"

Since in the old days there were many occasions in daily life when people were sitting formally i.e., on the knees, a great deal of consideration was given to applying techniques from that position.

The importance of studying *suwari waza* ("sitting techniques") nowadays is that it exercises the legs and hips and improves movement in a way that the study of *tachi waza* ("standing techniques") cannot.

Shikkō is the basic method of advancing or retiring while in a sitting or kneeling position. Care must be taken to maintain the correct upright posture throughout the movement.

● As one leg moves the body swivels on the knee of the other.

▶ Keep the hips down, rest the hands lightly on the thighs, and look directly at the front.

▲ Next, using the left knee as pivot, raise the right knee; move the feet 90° to the right (counter-clockwise) and thus take another pace forward.

● Keep the knees on the floor.

▲ From the *seiza* position with heels raised, lift the left knee and, pivoting on the right knee, swing both feet 90° in a clockwise direction, keeping them close together—thus taking a step forward.

▲ Without raising the right knee lower the left knee, which is pointing forward, to the ground.

10 Seiza-hō

"Moving into a formal sitting position"

Since one can compose one's mind by composing one's posture, it is very important that one maintain a correct posture between standing and sitting. *Seiza-hō* is the method of moving from a standing position to *seiza*.

3 ◄ Without moving the left foot place the right foot beside it and lower the hips.

1 ▶ Assume *migi-hanmi*.

4 ◄ Place both hands lightly on the thighs.

2
● The toes must not be extended backwards.

5 ◄ Push the knees forward and sit on the legs.

▲ Moving straight from *migi-hanmi* place the left knee beside the right heel.

6 ◄ Straighten the spine, draw the chin in, drop the shoulders and sit in *seiza*.

11 Ukemi
"Breakfalls"

Ukemi is a method of protecting the body when falling or being thrown. The techniques vary according to the angle and direction of the fall and the execution can vary with the individual. But the basic principle is to reduce the shock of the fall to the minimum.

● BACKWARD BREAKFALLS

▲ From a backward position start to lower the hips; at the same time extend both arms to the front at shoulder level.

▲ Curve the back and place the buttocks as close as possible to the heels.

◄ Roll to the rear, keeping the back curved and the chin pulled well in. Both arms remain relaxed but strike the mat strongly.

◄ Without bending the hips too much allow the body to assume the shape of a cradle, i.e., allow it to "rock"; keep the chin in to prevent the back of the head from striking the mat.

• FORWARD BREAKFALLS

This is the method of breaking one's fall when being thrown or falling forward.

1

2

▲ Advance the right hand and foot, inclining the body and allowing the weight of the body to move forward.

● The right hand should be placed on the mat as demonstrated in the photograph; the elbow should be slightly bent to give the feeling that the arm is describing an arc.

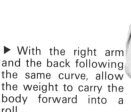

▶ With the right arm and the back following the same curve, allow the weight to carry the body forward into a roll.

● Keep the chin pulled in.

3

◀ As the roll goes over, the left arm strikes the mat strongly and the right leg should be bent almost 90° when it comes into contact with the ground.

4

◀ The momentum of the roll will bring the body back into an upright position. Correct the posture to meet any new attack.

● JUMPING BREAKFALLS

This method is used when it is impossible to free the appropriate hand and use the normal forward breakfall.

▲ Step forward onto the right foot, use it as a pivot and incline the body forward.

▶ Pull in the chin and launch the body high off the right foot, turning in mid-air.

▲ As the body turns over, the left leg remains straight and the left arm prepares to strike the mat in contact.

▲ As in the case of the normal forward breakfall, the momentum of the roll will bring the body back into an upright position.

◀ Correct the posture to prepare for the next movement.

There are a great many basic techniques but the study of those described in this section will provide an entrée to all aikido technique. The mysteries of *budō* are nowadays seldom kept secret. The movements described in this book provide the key to aikido; in other words "the secrets lie in the beginning."

When studying basic techniques, it is not sufficient to learn how to throw and control. It is necessary repeatedly to *be* thrown and controlled if one is to really understand and master the essentials of basic technique. Repeated and correct practice of these basic techniques eventually enables the *aikidoka* to react instinctively and to apply the appropriate technique in the situation in which he finds himself— whether it takes place in the *dōjō* or at an unexpected moment in daily life.

The figures (a) and (b) placed after the names of techniques are used to indicate when the opponent pulls (a) and when he pushes (b).

The photograph shows a moment in *irimi-nage*.

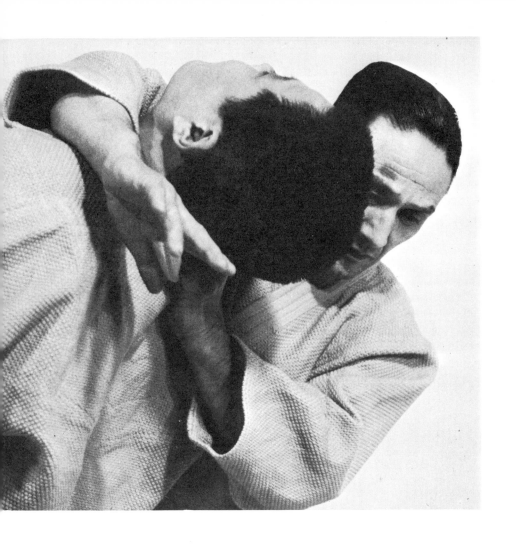

SECTION 3

Basic Techniques

SHIHŌ-NAGE
"Four-directions throw"

WHAT IS SHIHŌ-NAGE?

Shihō-nage is a technique in which the body movement is similar to that when using a sword and cutting in four directions. *Tori* turns pivoting on either foot and "folding" *uke's* arm i.e., taking his wrist to his shoulder. He thus controls him and is able to throw him in any other direction.

This book deals with only the basic forms of *shihō-nage — katate-mochi, yokomen-uchi, shōmen-uchi* and *hanmi-hantachi*. But there are many other forms of the technique such as *ryōte-mochi, hiji-mochi, mune-mochi, shōmen-tsuki, ushiro-ryōte-mochi* etc., and in addition there are all the variations of these techniques which are also forms of *shihō-nage*. When applying *shihō-nage* all the basic movements come into use including the basic movements of *shūmatsu dōsa*.

● *Points to Remember*

It is important when practicing *shihō-nage* to think in terms of using a sword: raising a sword, wheeling with a sword, cutting downward with a sword. Furthermore, it is important to feel that you are applying your strength in the most effective direction to control your opponent, not merely twisting his wrist. Instead of using simply the strength of one hand the *aikidoka* must put all his body into the movement. *Uke's* hand must move in a line with the shoulder: *tori* must not pull *uke's* hand out to the side.

Katate-mochi Shihō-nage *(A)*
"One hand grasp; four-directions throw"

This technique is used when *uke* grasps one of *tori's* wrists and pulls.
The movement is the same as in *shūmatsu-dōsa* (Page 36).

◀ In *migi-gyaku-hanmi*, *uke* grasps *tori's* left wrist and pulls him forward.

● Tori extends his right arm as far as possible.

▲ After applying *atemi* (*metsubushi*) with the right hand *tori* moves in exactly the same manner as in *shūmatsu-dōsa* 1.

▲ Taking a big pace with his left foot, *tori* raises *uke's* hand above *tori's* head.

▲ Pivoting on both feet *tori* turns 180° and takes *uke's* right hand to his (*uke's*) right shoulder.

7

◄ *Tori* follows *uke* down bringing his right foot close to *uke's* right shoulder and kneeling on the left knee close to his (*tori's*) right heel. With his right hand he holds *uke's* wrist firmly against the mat and with the left hand applies *atemi* to *uke's* face.

● Throughout the whole movement *tori's* eyes must stay on *uke* and he must be careful to maintain the correct posture.

5

6

▲ *Tori* takes another pace forward with his right foot (*suri-ashi*) and, throwing his weight forward, breaks *uke's* balance to the rear

▲ *Tori* brings *uke* to the ground with a downward cutting motion of the right hand.

BASIC TECHNIQUES **51**

Katate-mochi Shihō-nage *(B)*
"One hand grasp; four-directions throw"

This technique is used when *uke* grasps *tori's* wrist and pushes.

● Apply *atemi* positively.
● To avoid injury *uke* must receive the blow on his left hand.

▶ In *hidari-gyaku-hanmi*, when *uke* grasps *tori's* left wrist and pushes, *tori* applies *atemi* (*metsubushi*) with the right hand.

● Do not resist *uke's* push.

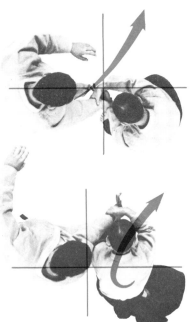

◆ Without resisting *uke's* push, *tori* pivots on his forward foot and, while beginning to withdraw his right foot to the rear, grasps *uke's* wrist with his right hand.

◆ While lowering his body weight *tori* turns clockwise to the rear.

4

◀ Still pivoting on his left foot, *tori* turns 180° and brings his weight over his left foot, stabilizing his posture.

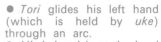
- *Tori* glides his left hand (which is held by *uke*) through an arc.
- *Uke's* hand is at the level of *tori's* shoulder.
- Tori extends his left hand to the front.

5

◆ *Tori* grasps *uke's* wrist so that his thumb is on *uke's* pulse.

6

◆ *Tori*, without changing the position of his feet and while quickly turning his body 180°, raises his hands above his head—again as though wielding a sword.

7

◆ The turn is completed and from here on the movements are the same as those in *shihō-nage* (a).

3 Yokomen-uchi Shihō-nage *(A)*
"Blow to side of head; four-directions throw"

When the opponent attacks with a sideways blow to the head, his power is used to break his balance and he is thrown with *shihō-nage.*

▶ In *migi-hanmi, uke* strikes at the left side of *tori's* head with the side of his right hand (*tegatana*). *Tori* steps forward half a pace diagonally to his right, slightly "opening" his left foot.

▲ *Tori* strikes down *uke's* right arm with the edge of his left hand (*tegatana*) and at the same time applies *atemi* to *uke's* face with the back of his right fist.

▲ *Tori* grasps *uke's* right wrist with both hands. (Thumb and fingers of the left hand are close on the pad at the base of *uke's* thumb and *tori's* right thumb is on *uke's* pulse.)

TORI UKE

● The feet should move by *suri-ashi* and care must be taken to keep them at 90° to each other as if in the basic posture (*kamae*).

▶ As in *kata-mochi shihō-nage* (Page 50), *tori* turns and, straightening the arms, takes *uke* backward to the ground and applies *atemi*.

▲ Taking a half-pace forward with the right foot and twisting his hips to bring them square to the front, *tori* pushes the hands forward and breaks *uke's* balance.

◀ *Tori* takes a long step forward with his left foot and raises the hands level with his forehead.

● At this point *tori's* left hand guides *uke's* hands forward and his right hand secures the lock on *uke's* wrist with a twisting movement.

turn through **180°**

turn through **180°**

● If the posture is stable the feet need only move a short distance to be effective.

4 Yokomen-uchi Shihō-nage *(B)*
"Blow to side of head; four-directions throw"

▲ In *hidari-gyaku-hanmi*, *uke* raises his right arm to attack with a blow to the side of the head. At this moment *tori* steps forward with the left foot.

▲ *Tori* forestalls the attack by striking down *uke's* right arm with his left hand (*tegatana*), at the same time applying *atemi* (*metsubushi*).

5 Shōmen-uchi Shihō-nage *(B)*
"Straight blow; four-directions throw"

▲ In *migi-ai-hanmi*, when *uke* attacks by making a straight cut to the head with his right hand, *tori* deflects the blow, grasps *uke's* wrist with his left and "opening" his body to the rear, breaks *uke's* posture.

▲ Still grasping *uke's* wrist (*tori's* thumb lies across the pad at the base of *uke's* thumb), *tori* applies *atemi* with his right hand (*metsubushi*).

When *uke* attacks with a blow to the side of the head, *tori* takes the initiative by stepping in and securing *uke's* wrist and applying *shihō-nage*.

▲ *Tori* grasps *uke's* right arm with both hands and, pivoting on the left foot, sweeps his right foot round to the rear.

▲ Having broken *uke's* balance, *tori* turns (clockwise) 180° transferring his weight from the left to the right foot and applies *shihō-nage*.

When the opponent attacks with a straight blow to the head, *tori* deflects the blow, breaks the opponent's balance and applies *shihō-nage*.

▲ When *uke* attempts to block the *atemi* with his left hand, *tori* grasps *uke's* wrist with both hands, takes half a pace to the front with his left foot, squares his hips and thrusts his hands forward.

▲ Taking a big step forward with his left foot, *tori* raises his hands above his head, breaking *uke's* posture, and immediately turns 180° to apply *shihō-nage*.

6 Hanmi-hantachi Katate-mochi Shihō-nage
"One sitting, one standing; one hand grasp; four-directions throw"

When *uke* grasps *tori's* wrist, *tori* secures *uke's* wrist
and applies *shihō-nage* from a sitting position.

1

● *Tori* thrusts forward with an upward circular movement as if to scrape *uke's* left knee with the little finger of his right hand.

◀ *Tori* is in *seiza*, and *uke*, approaching from the side, grasps *tori's* right hand with his left.

● *Tori* moves forward so that *uke's* shoulder is above *tori's* head and *tori* can see forward under *uke's* arm.
● At the same time *tori* raises the toes of both feet, brings the heels together and firmly settles his weight down upon them.

2

3

▲ Synchronizing his movement with *uke's* pull, *tori* quickly advances his right knee to a position about one-third of the distance between *uke's* feet and grasps *uke's* wrist at chest height.

▲ While transferring his weight from the front to the rear and with the action of raising a sword, *tori* secures the lock on *uke's* wrist and elbow and breaks his balance to *uke's* left rear.

6

• Keep the arm straight.
• Move the knees correctly.

▶ *Tori*, while sitting, throws *uke* backwards.

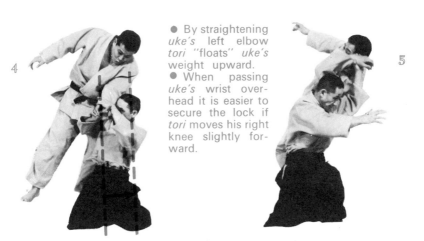

4

• By straightening *uke's* left elbow *tori* "floats" *uke's* weight upward.
• When passing *uke's* wrist overhead it is easier to secure the lock if *tori* moves his right knee slightly forward.

5

▲ *Tori* transfers his weight more and more onto his left knee and at the same time raises his hands over his head.

▲ Once *uke's* balance is broken, *tori* passes *uke's* wrist over his head, moving *uke* round behind him. And then, turning his hips, *tori* brings *uke's* left hand to his left shoulder.

Hanmi-hantachi Ryōte-mochi Shihō-nage

"One sitting, one standing; both hands grasp; four-directions throw"

Uke approaches tori, who is sitting, from the front, grasps both wrists and pulls. Tori comes to his feet, takes uke's wrist over his head and applies shihō-nage.

1

▲ Tori is in seiza; uke, in migi-hanmi, grasps both tori's wrists from the front and pulls.

2

3

▶ Tori comes to his feet stretching upward with his hands, before bringing them over his head.

▲ Tori comes onto his left foot and advances it between uke's feet; still with his right knee on the ground he thrusts uke's hands forward at chest level, holding uke's right wrist with his right hand.

● Tori is up on his right toes.
● Tori's left hand moves directly forward.

4

▶ As he passes uke's hands over his head tori turns (clockwise) 180° and pivoting on the left foot, takes a big step forward (to uke's rear) with his right foot, throwing uke with shihō-nage.

● Tori's right arm must be straight.
● Tori's hips must be lowered if he is to break uke's balance.

● AIKIDO TECHNIQUE

Aikido can be divided into *suwari waza* (both *tori* and *uke* are sitting), *hanmi-hantachi waza* (one sitting, the other standing) and *tachi waza* (both standing); and these are further divided into *nage waza* (throwing techniques) and *osae waza* (controlling techniques).

It is also possible to divide the techniques into those that exploit physiological weakpoints and those that take advantage of the position and movement of the opponent. Examples of the former are the targets we attack with *atemi* to cause unexpected shock and leave the opponent vulnerable. An example of the latter is the power of the opponent's pushing and pulling movements which can be harnessed.

Aikido is the study of how to obtain the maximum effect with the expenditure of a small amount of effort. Any technique that has to be forced or involves a contest of strength is not aikido.

It is true of *osae waza*, and particularly true of *nage waza*, that to throw an opponent it is not necessary to have the strength to lift him. It is essential that the opponent is thrown of his own accord. (Failure to "go over" would mean that the joint would be broken.)

The question of how best an opponent can be defeated must always be in one's mind—but it is of supreme importance to reflect upon the correctness of one's own movement and attitude.

IKKAJŌ OSAE
"1st control"

WHAT IS IKKAJŌ OSAE?

Ikkajō osae is a method of breaking an opponent's posture and controlling him by a movement that centers on the elbow joint. As with *shihō-nage* there are many variations of this movement—*katate-mochi, ryōte-mochi, hiji-mochi, mune-mochi, shōmen-tsuki* etc.—but the basic movements are *shōmen-uchi* and *katate-mochi* which are explained.

● *Points to Remember*
Application of this technique embodies movements such as raising the sword, cutting downward, thrusting as though with a spear, advancing "into" an opponent (*irimi*), etc. For *tori* the technique is an excellent method of learning to judge the distance between oneself and an opponent

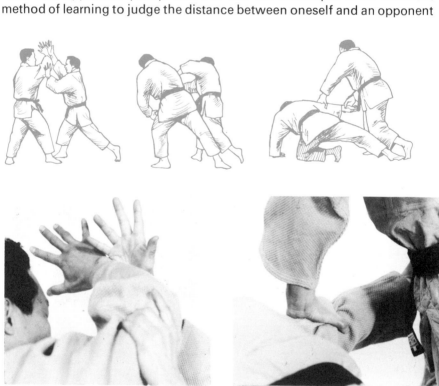

(*maai*), advancing diagonally, hip movement and chaneling power etc. Performance of the technique enables *uke* to practice forward breakfalls and to strengthen the wrist, elbow and shoulder joints which in turn benefits application of the technique.

In *suwari waza* (sitting techniques) it is important that both *tori* and *uke's* vision be correct and at the beginning of the movement they must be sitting on the toes with the feet together. This posture makes for easy movement and allows power to be applied quickly in all *suwari waza*. Sitting correctly strengthens the legs and hips.

Shōmen-uchi Ikkajō Osae *(A)*
"Straight blow; 1st control"

- *Uke* receives *tori's* blow with his right arm slightly curved.

1

Tori attacks with a downward blow to the head from the front and *uke* blocks the blow with his right hand; *tori* seizes *uke's* right elbow and wrist and brings him to the ground and under control.

◀ In *migi-ai-hanmi*, *tori* raises his right hand above his head as if raising a sword, advances with *suri-ashi* and delivers a blow to *uke's* head directly from the front and with the edge of the hand (*tegatana*).

▼ While pushing *uke's* elbow along a line joining the point of his right shoulder to his right ear, *tori's* right *tegatana* cuts downward with a circular movement and he steps diagonally to the right with the left foot following slightly.

2

▼ *Tori* advances his right foot; turns his hips sharply to the right; brings his left hand down sharply on *uke's* elbow joint.

3

- Use *suri-ashi* when moving.
- Move quickly to keep the initiative.

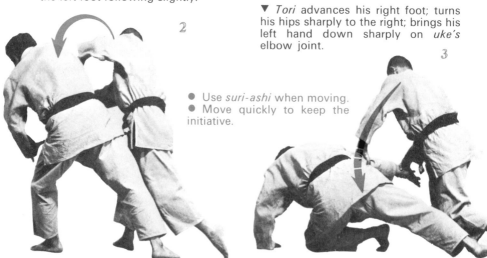

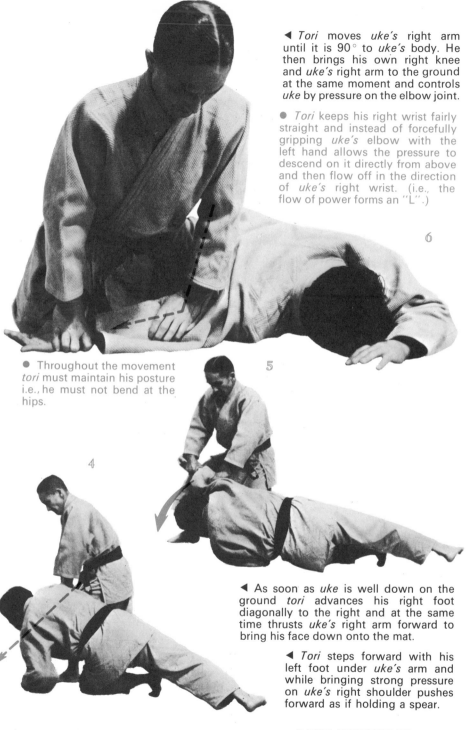

◀ *Tori* moves *uke's* right arm until it is 90° to *uke's* body. He then brings his own right knee and *uke's* right arm to the ground at the same moment and controls *uke* by pressure on the elbow joint.

● *Tori* keeps his right wrist fairly straight and instead of forcefully gripping *uke's* elbow with the left hand allows the pressure to descend on it directly from above and then flow off in the direction of *uke's* right wrist. (i.e., the flow of power forms an "L".)

6

● Throughout the movement *tori* must maintain his posture i.e., he must not bend at the hips.

5

4

◀ As soon as *uke* is well down on the ground *tori* advances his right foot diagonally to the right and at the same time thrusts *uke's* right arm forward to bring his face down onto the mat.

◀ *Tori* steps forward with his left foot under *uke's* arm and while bringing strong pressure on *uke's* right shoulder pushes forward as if holding a spear.

2 Shōmen-uchi Ikkajō Osae (A—sitting)
"Shoulder grasp; 1st control"

This is the same as the previous movement except that both *tori* and *uke* are in *seiza* ("sitting"). When in *seiza* the distance between the knees should be the width of one fist, the chest should be thrown out and the shoulders relaxed.

● When facing each other the distance between *tori's* and *uke's* knees should be the width of two fists.

● The big toes should overlap.
● Keep the chest out and drop the shoulders.

▲ Both in *seiza, tori* strikes downward and directly from the front toward *uke's* head. *Uke* blocks the blow with his right hand and *tori* immediately seizes his right elbow from below.

▶ Coming up onto his toes, *tori* moves the right knee slightly forward and while making a curved downward movement with the right *tegatana*, pushes strongly upward at the right side with his left hand which is holding *uke's* right elbow. *Uke's* posture is now broken.

▶ *Tori* controls *uke* by pushing his arm as if to force it lengthways into the point of the shoulders; at the same time moving the left knee up to below *uke's* shoulder *tori* advances his right knee diagonally to the right and secures *ikkajō osae*.

● The knees must not lose contact with the ground when moving and the heels should remain close together.

4

▶ By lowering the hips and bringing pressure to bear on *uke's* right elbow from above, *tori* breaks *uke's* posture completely.

● *Tori* must be careful not to prevent the securing of *uke's* right arm by reducing the *maai* too much.

3

● *Tori* must not concentrate so much on grasping *uke's* right wrist but rather on cutting downward strongly with the right *tegatana*.

◀ Turning the hips firmly to the right and cutting downward with the right hand, *tori* grasps *uke's* right wrist in front of his (*tori's*) right thigh.

BASIC TECHNIQUES 67

3 Kata-mochi Ikkajō Osae *(A)*
"Shoulder grasp; 1st control"

When *uke* seizes *tori* at the shoulder, *tori* by concentrating his strength (*shūchū-ryoku*) in that region, secures *uke's* elbow and subdues him.

◀ In *hidari-hanmi, uke* seizes *tori's* right shoulder and pulls; *tori* applies *atemi* (*metsubushi*) and takes a pace diagonally to the right rear with his right foot.

After the blow *tori* grasps *uke's* left wrist with the same hand and applies his right hand against *uke's* arm from below.

● *Tori* must concentrate his power in the region of *uke's* grip but not raise the shoulders.

◀ *Tori* takes a pace forward with his left foot and with right *tegatana* pushes upward and forward along a line joining *uke's* shoulder and ear.

4

● Change from right *tegatana* and grip *uke's* elbow from above.

◄ Twist hips strongly to the left and with right *tegatana* direct a downward blow to *uke's* elbow joint and shift the weight to the left leg.

5

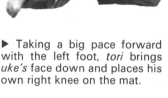

◄ Without loosening his grip on *uke's* shoulder or wrist, *tori* pushes strongly forward to the right and at the same time slides his right foot from *uke's* left side toward his right shoulder.

6

► Taking a big pace forward with the left foot, *tori* brings *uke's* face down and places his own right knee on the mat.

7

◄ Placing his right knee below *uke's* left shoulder and opening *uke's* left arm to an angle of 90°, *tori* brings both *uke's* elbow and wrist firmly down onto the mat and controls *uke*.

● When securing *uke's* arm *tori* should bend *uke's* wrist in the direction of the shoulder as soon as it has touched the mat.

4 Kata-mochi Ikkajō Osae *(A—sitting)* "Shoulder grasp; 1st control"

● *Uke's* left hand should be palm downward.

▶ Both in *seiza, uke* grasps *tori's* right shoulder with his left hand and pulls.

▶ To evade the full force of *uke's* attack, *tori* shifts his right knee to the right, comes up on his toes and with his left hand applies *atemi* (*metsubushi*).

● *Tori* moves as if to thrust the right shoulder and right *tegatana* forward.

▶ *Tori* grasps *uke's* left hand which is gripping *tori's* right shoulder and holds it in as if to bind the back of *uke's* hand to the shoulder. He advances his left knee diagonally left and applying right *tegatana* to *uke's* elbow, pushes upward along a line joining *uke's* shoulder and ear.

▶ *Tori* now cuts sharply down with *tegatana*, and at the same time turns the hips to the left.

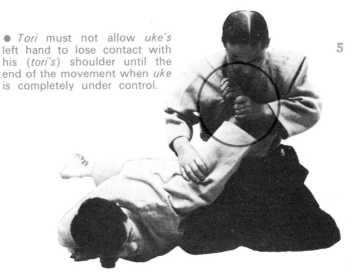

● *Tori* must not allow *uke's* left hand to lose contact with his (*tori's*) shoulder until the end of the movement when *uke* is completely under control.

▲ *Tori* now grips *uke's* elbow with his right hand and pushes diagonally to the right; he places his right knee below *uke's* left shoulder to complete the movement.

In aikido, in addition to developing and training the physique, great stress is laid on developing *shūchū-ryoku*—the concentration of attention and strength at one point when applying a technique. This version of *kata-mochi ikkajō-osae* is an ideal technique for cultivating both; it requires the application of *shūchū-ryoku* in the region of the shoulder and, like all *suwari waza*, it develops the legs and hips and demands fast, subtle movement.

5 Kata-mochi Ikkajō Osae *(B)* "Shoulder grasp; 1st control"

● When pushing upward with the right *tegatana* the right shoulder must be advanced.

▲ In *gyaku-hanmi*, *uke* grasps *tori's* right shoulder with his left hand and pushes. *Tori* applies *atemi* (*metsubushi*) with the left hand and advances his right foot diagonally.

▲ With his left hand *tori* clamps *uke's* left hand to his (*tori's*) shoulder and with right *tegatana* pushes *uke's* left elbow strongly upward, at the same time opening his left foot slightly.

6 Kata-mochi Ikkajō Osae *(B—sitting)* "Straight blow; 1st control"

▼ Both are in *seiza* when *uke* seizes *tori's* right shoulder with his left hand (palm downward). *Tori* opens his right knee and applies *atemi* (*metsubushi*) with his left hand.

▼ *Tori's* left hand grasps *uke's* right wrist and while pushing *uke's* left elbow strongly upward with *tegatana*, he moves slightly to the rear.

● The *tegatana* must be executed along a line connecting the knees, hips and face.

This version of the throw is applied when *uke* grasps the shoulder and pushes.

● Strike sideways with *te-gatana*.

4 5 6

▲ Bringing his left foot around behind him in a big sweep *tori* turns 180° and brings his right *tegatana* down strongly, at the same time lowering the body.

▲ *Tori* comes down onto his right knee, brings *uke* face downward onto the mat and skewering the elbow applies *ikkajō osae*.

Example of the above movement.

▼ Making a big sweep to the rear with his left knee, *tori* turns 180° bringing the right *tegatana* strongly downward and completely breaking *uke's* posture forward.

▼ Bringing *uke's* face downward onto the mat, *tori* immobilizes him as in the previous technique.

4

5

NIKAJŌ OSAE
"2nd control"

WHAT IS NIKAJŌ OSAE?

Nikajō is a technique directed at the elbow and the wrist and can be used to inflict much pain if applied skillfully. Consequently many beginners give up before they have mastered this technique; but constant practice helps the student build up considerable tolerance to pain and makes him less vulnerable to wrist techniques. Furthermore, since it stretches and softens the sinews not used in everyday life and at the same time stimulates the nerve endings, the practice of *nikajō* is beneficial to the health.

There are countless situations in which *nikajō* can be used, as there are with all the other basic techniques. Here the descriptions will be confined to *katate-mochi* and *kata-mochi*, i.e., the techniques used when gripped by an opponent.

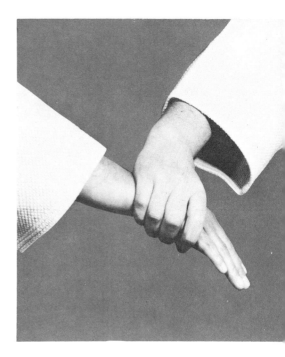

● Points to Remember

Although *nikajō* is a method of grasping the opponent's hand it does not depend simply upon a powerful grip. Rather, the technique depends upon the same principles followed when holding a sword: the grip is exerted mainly through the little fingers, both hands are used, and *uke's* wrist is held in the same position and at the same angle as *tori* would hold a sword if the intention were to cut down *uke* from the front.

When applying the technique the strength of the whole body—not just the upper part—must be concentrated on *uke's* wrist. If the basic movements of the feet, the use of the weight and the hips are not correct then *nikajō* cannot be effective.

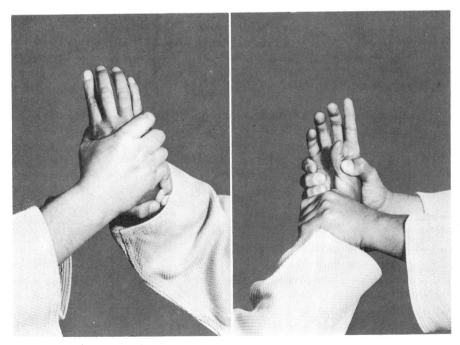

Katate-mochi Nikajō Osae (A)
"One hand grasp; 2nd control"

▲ In left *ai-hanmi*, *uke* grasps *tori's* right wrist with his left hand. *Tori* moves his right hand to his right side (palm downward), moves his right foot to the right (*suri-ashi*) and applies *atemi* with his left hand (*metsubushi*).

▲ *Tori* brings *uke's* hand over to point directly in front and level with *tori's* eyes and, grasping *uke's* wrist with his right hand, grips *uke's* hand across the back with his left.

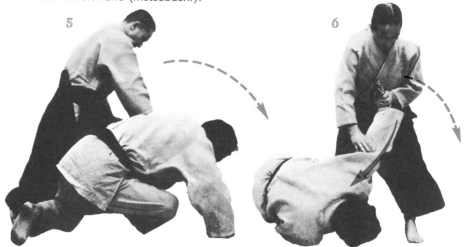

▲ *Tori* takes a pace with his right foot along a line running from below *uke's* arm to the point of his shoulder and, securing *uke's* arm, pushes him forward.

▲ *Tori* maintains control of *uke's* arm by pushing it toward the point of *uke's* shoulder and advancing one pace diagonally to the left brings *uke's* face down toward the mat.

This movement involves the application of *ikkajō* on *uke's* wrist: when *uke* grabs *tori* with one hand and pulls, *tori* applies *ikkajō* on *uke's* wrist.

3

▲ With a downward stroke of both hands in the direction of *uke's* left side and bringing his weight forward, *tori* secures *uke's* wrist.

4

▲ While advancing still further with the left foot, *tori* grips *uke's* elbow with his right hand and, pushing downward, turns his hips to the left.

7

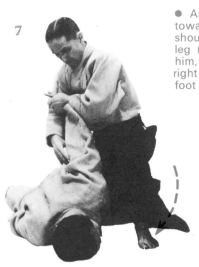

● As *tori* turns in toward *uke* he should draw the left leg (still bent) with him, pivoting on the right knee. The right foot is up on its toes.

8

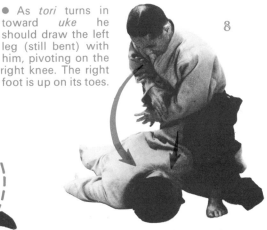

▲ *Tori* comes down onto his right knee to bring *uke* completely face downward.

▲ *Tori* brings his left foot up close to *uke's* face so that his body is at 90° to *uke's*. He holds *uke's* left wrist in the crook of his right elbow and presses his (*tori's*) right arm against his own chest. With left *tegatana tori* secures *uke's* left elbow.

Katate-mochi Nikajō Osae (A)

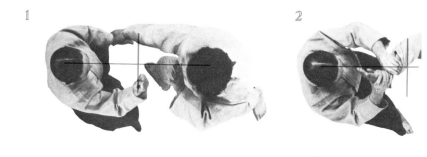

● There are no movements in aikido that follow a straight line: the body and arms should always be describing an arc. In fact *tori's* movement is analogous to a whirlpool, with his body at the center which pulls in his opponent.

These photographs are of a reverse form of the previous technique: in this case, starting from *migi-ai-hanmi*, *uke* grasps *tori* with his right hand. But regardless of whether the attack comes from the left or the right side, the ensuing movements are exactly the same.

All aikido movements should be practiced from both sides.

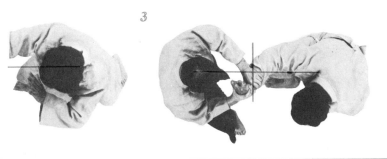

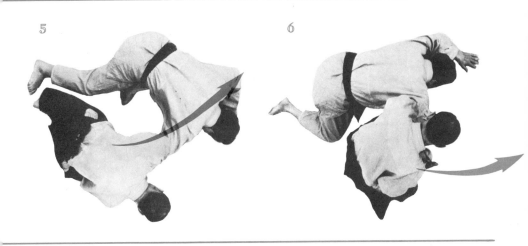

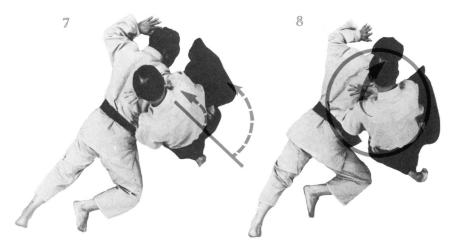

2 Katate-mochi Nikajō Osae *(A—sitting)* "One hand grasp; 2nd control"

Example of the previous movement when both are sitting.

3

1

▲ *Tori* now brings both hands down as if making a sword stroke and secures the wrist.

● Throughout the movement *tori* is up on his toes.

4

▲ *Uke* grasps *tori's* right wrist with his left hand. *Tori* moves his right hand to the right, takes his right knee slightly back and to the side. At the same time he applies *atemi* with his left hand.

▲ *Tori* grips *uke's* left elbow with his right hand and in the manner of *ikkajō* advances his left knee and breaks *uke's* posture.

2

5

▲ *Tori* advances his left knee diagonally to the left; with his right hand he grasps *uke's* wrist. *Tori's* left hand then grips *uke's* left hand in *nikajō*.

▲ Thrusting *uke's* arm forward, *tori* advances his right knee in the direction of *uke's* right shoulder, and, moving his left knee forward, is in a position to bring *uke* under complete control.

3 Katate-mochi Nikajō Osae *(B)*
''One hand grasp; 2nd control''

When *uke* grasps one hand and pushes, *tori* opens his body and applies *nikajō*.

▶ From *hidari-gyaku-hanmi, uke* grasps *tori's* right wrist with his left hand and pushes.

▶ *Tori* spreads his fingers and, lowering his hand to the right, steps to the right side with his right foot and applies *atemi (metsubushi)* with his left hand.

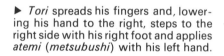

▶ Sweeping his left foot to the rear *tori* opens his body about 45° to the left and gripping *uke's* left wrist with his right hand brings it up level with his eyes; at the same time he grasps *uke's* hand with his left hand in the manner of *nikajō*.

▼ Without loosening the grip of the left hand and grasping *uke's* left elbow with his right hand, *tori*, with a circular sweeping movement, takes his left foot to the rear.

4

▶ Cutting down sharply with both hands to a point just below *uke's* left shoulder, *tori* secures *uke's* wrist.

● The weight of the body should be taken on both legs and the power should be concentrated in the big toe of the right foot.

5

6

▲ While pivoting on his left foot and turning 180° to the rear, *tori* opens his body widely to the left and at the same time cuts downward with both hands.

7

▶ Turning his hips sharply to the left he brings *uke* still lower. (*Uke* is brought to the ground in a sweeping movement around *tori's* right knee.)

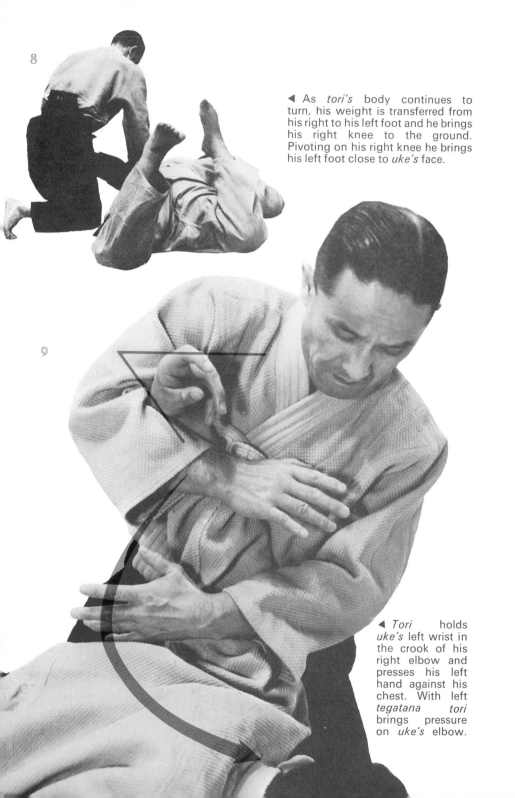

8

◄ As *tori's* body continues to turn, his weight is transferred from his right to his left foot and he brings his right knee to the ground. Pivoting on his right knee he brings his left foot close to *uke's* face.

9

◄ *Tori* holds *uke's* left wrist in the crook of his right elbow and presses his left hand against his chest. With left *tegatana tori* brings pressure on *uke's* elbow.

Kata-mochi Nikajō Osae (A)
"Shoulder grab; 2nd control"

● From *hidari-ai-hanmi*, *uke* grasps *tori's* right shoulder, with the left hand palm downward, and pulls.

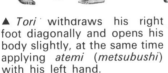

▲ *Tori* withdraws his right foot diagonally and opens his body slightly, at the same time applying *atemi* (*metsubushi*) with his left hand.

▲ *Tori* grips *uke's* left hand from above with his left hand, holds it firmly to his shoulder and, with right *tegatana*, pushes *uke's* elbow sharply upward.

Kata-mochi Nikajō Osae (A—sitting)
"Shoulder grab; 2nd control"

▲ Both are in *seiza*: *uke* grasps *tori's* right shoulder with his left hand palm downward. *Tori* immediately moves his right hand (palm upward) and his right knee to the right while applying *atemi* with his left hand.

▲ With his left hand *tori* grasps *uke's* left wrist from above and thrusts *uke's* elbow upward with right *tegatana*; while sliding the left knee forward *tori* secures *nikajō* pushing directly downward.

This technique is the application of *nikajō* while concentrating one's power in the shoulder. But the techniques must not be applied with the strength of the arms alone: the aim must be to utilize the movement of shoulder, arms and weight simultaneously. In other words, power must be concentrated along a single line.

▲ *Tori* holds *uke's* wrist firmly to his shoulder, applies *nikajō* and drives *uke's* elbow downward in the direction of his (*uke's*) left side.

▲ Without loosening the lock on *uke's* wrist, *tori* now grips *uke's* elbow with his right hand and, stepping forward with his left foot, turns his hips.

▲ *Tori* advances his right foot, pushes the secured arm toward the point of the shoulder and controls *uke.*

▲ Grasping *uke's* elbow with his right hand and moving his left knee forward, *tori* pushes *uke's* elbow sharply upward and then directly downward, breaking *uke's* posture diagonally to *tori's* right.

▲ Advancing his right knee along the line joining the base of *uke's* left shoulder and the point of his right, *tori* pushes *uke's* arm in the direction of the shoulder and brings *uke* over onto his face to control him.

6 Kata-mochi Nikajō Osae (B—sitting)
"Shoulder grab; 2nd control"

Both are in *seiza* when *uke* grasps *tori's* shoulder and pushes. *Tori* applies *nikajō* and making a big turn brings *uke* under control.

▲ *Uke* grasps *tori's* right shoulder with the left hand palm downward. *Tori* comes up onto his toes (without allowing his weight to float), moves his right knee slightly to the right and applies *atemi* with the left hand.

● *Tori* must never relax the grip of his left hand.
● *Tori*, when pushing upward with *tegatana*, must never allow *uke's* hand to lose contact with his shoulder.

▲ Dropping the left knee slightly to the rear, *tori's* left hand grasps *uke's* wrist in the *nikajō* position and at the same time, *tori* pushes *uke's* elbow upward using right *tegatana*.

▶ Without allowing *uke's* left hand to move (which is held fast to *tori's* shoulder), *tori* brings the *tegatana* directly downward and applies *nikajō* by pushing in the direction of *uke's* shoulder.

4

◀ Grasping *uke's* elbow with his right hand and still holding *uke's* wrist in the *nikajō* position, *tori* makes a counter-clockwise sweep to the rear with his left foot, turning his body and hands 180°.

◀ *Tori's* hands push downward as he turns, bringing *uke* face downward to the ground.

5

▼ Transferring his weight from the right to the left knee and turning the hips sharply, *tori* pushes *uke's* elbow down further and brings him under control.

6

SANKAJŌ
"3rd control"

WHAT IS SANKAJŌ?

This basic technique—which strengthens the elbows and wrists—is a method of securing the opponent's wrist in a "hook shape."

As with *ikkajō* and *nikajō*, *sankajō* is not merely a controlling technique: it can also be used to throw an opponent. Space limits the number of *sankajō* controlling techniques that can be included in this book but, in addition to those mentioned here, there are *katate-mochi, ryōte-mochi, yokomen-uchi, hiji-mochi, shōmen-tsuki*, all the techniques used when attacked from behind and all the variations.

The study of this group of techniques is of course of great benefit to *tori*. But, as with other techniques, practice is also useful for *uke:* in

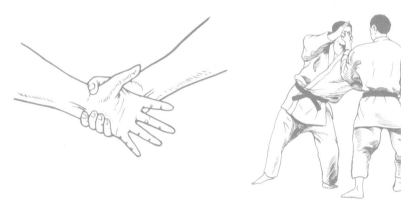

addition to strengthening the wrists and elbows, knowledge of *uke's* reactions are valuable when it comes to apply the technique.

● *Points to Remember*

In all martial arts, aikido no less, the wrists and elbows are toughened to apply *atemi* effectively and to meet the opponent's attack.

There are numerous aikido techniques which include the use of *atemi* and there is no comparison in the effect of blows delivered by "tempered" and "untempered" hands.

Taking the part of both *tori* and *uke* produces strong and supple joints, adds to the individual's speed and ability to concentrate power and develops positive strength. Accordingly, since experiencing pain and building up tolerance has a direct connection with strengthening oneself as a whole, it is especially necessary for both *uke* and *tori* to cooperate in practicing correctly the major techniques.

● *Suwari waza ("sitting techniques")*

Ikkajō, nikajō, sankajō, yonkajō (described later) and many other aikido techniques are practiced in a sitting position. This is because the samurai spent a great deal of time indoors sitting formally and thus had to be able

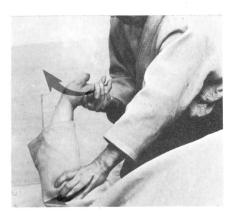
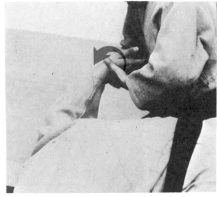

to defend themselves in these circumstances.

Movements made in a sitting position make greater demands on the body than standing techniques and to be fast calls for strong and supple legs. The samurai discovered that the performance of sitting techniques greatly benefited the performance of standing techniques. As a result, though *suwari waza* were harder they were practiced as much as—or even more than *tachi waza*.

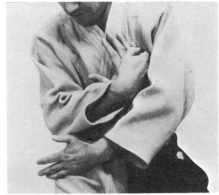

Shōmen-uchi Sankajō Osae *(B)*
"Straight blow; 3rd control"

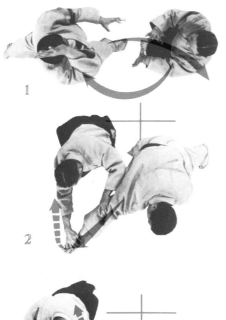

When *uke* attacks with a blow to the head, *tori* moves to one side as in *nikajō osae* (b), and applies *sankajō*.

● By studying these photographs taken from above in conjunction with those of the following pages, one can appreciate the smooth, circular movement which is the special feature of aikido.

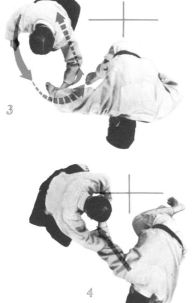

◀ In *hidari-gyaku-hanmi*, *uke* attacks from the front with *tegatana*.

◀ While deflecting the blow, *tori* very quickly makes a 180° turn toward *uke's* right rear, destroying his posture.

● *Tori* grips *uke's* upper arm with his left hand.

▲ Grasping the fingers of *uke's* right hand, *tori* pushes them directly upward keeping *uke* off-balance while he changes his grip.

▲ With his left hand *tori* applies *sankajō*.

5

◀ While maintaining the *sankajō* and thus causing *uke* to "float" his weight, *tori* grasps *uke's* right elbow with his right hand.

6

◀ Securing both *uke's* wrist and elbow, *tori* pulls strongly down toward his own hips.

● The lock is secured by "straightening" *uke's* elbow i.e., by pressing against the joint.

7

▶ While pulling, *tori* again turns 180 degrees clockwise whirling *uke* around and down onto the mat.

● Be careful not to loosen the grip on *uke's* wrist.

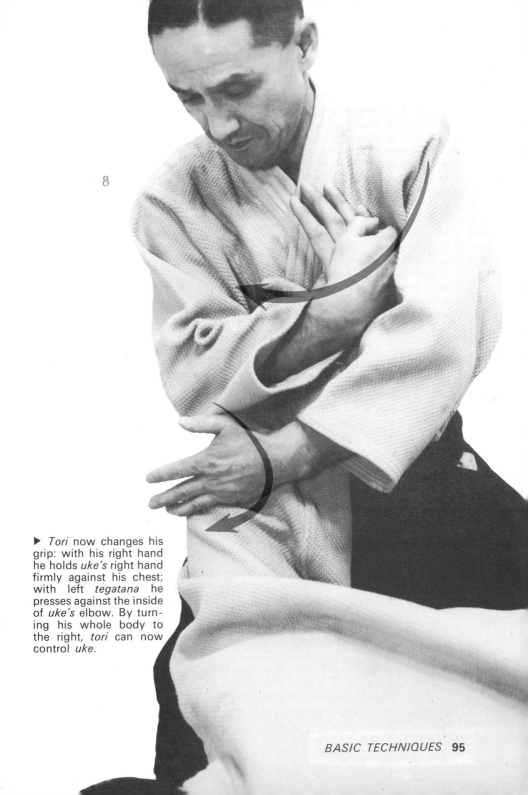

▶ *Tori* now changes his grip: with his right hand he holds *uke's* right hand firmly against his chest; with left *tegatana* he presses against the inside of *uke's* elbow. By turning his whole body to the right, *tori* can now control *uke*.

Shōmen-uchi Sankajō Osae (B—sitting)
"Straight blow; 3rd control"

Sankajō applied against a blow to the face when both are sitting.

▲ Both are in *seiza* and *uke* attacks with right *tegatana* to the head. *Tori* deflects the blow with right *tegatana*, at the same time grasping *uke's* elbow as if to "float" his weight upward.

▲ Still sitting and using the left knee as a pivot, *tori* turns (clockwise) 180°, breaking *uke's* posture and at the same time grasping his fingers.

▲ While pulling *uke's* right arm strongly with his left hand, *tori* applies *atemi* with his right.

▲ As soon as he has applied *atemi*, *tori* grasps *uke's* right elbow.

▲ Using both hands, *tori* pulls strongly downward bringing *uke* down onto the mat.

3 ▲ *Tori's* right hand holding *uke's* fingers pushes upward; his left hand under *uke's* elbow also helps to keep *uke* off-balance by pushing in the same direction.

4 ▲ *Tori* applies *sankaiō* with the left hand.

8 ▲ *Tori* adjusts the angle of his body and secures *uke's* arm.

● *Tori* takes advantage of his unbalanced opponent.

9 ▲ *Tori* brings *uke* under complete control.

3 Mune-mochi Sankajō Osae *(B)*
"Chest grasp; 3rd control"

When *uke* grasps *tori* by the lapel, *tori* passes under
uke's arm and applies *sankajō*.

◀ In *ai-hanmi*, *uke* grasps
tori's lapel.

▼ Utilizing the force of *uke's* push,
tori moves his body to the left and
applies *atemi* (*metsubushi*) with
his right hand.

▼ While *uke* is reacting to the *atemi*,
tori lowers his body and passes
under *uke's* arm.

● While passing under *uke's* arm,
with his left hand *tori* grips *uke's*
right hand from the back.

▶ *Tori* turns toward *uke* and with *uke's* hand held firmly against the chest, applies *sankajō*. From this point the movement is the same as *shōmen-uchi sankajō* (b).

6

▶ Pressing *uke's* right hand firmly against his chest, *tori* transfers his weight to his left foot and turns his upper body coun-ter-clock-wise 180°.

5

4

● While moving past *uke*, *tori* applies *atemi* with his right elbow against the side of *uke's* chest.

◀ When passing under *uke's* arm, *tori's* weight is kept forward. *Tori* grasps *uke's* right hand and keeps it firmly against his chest.

YONKAJŌ OSAE
"4th control"

WHAT IS YONKAJŌ OSAE?

This technique is directed against the inside of the opponent's wrist. If applied correctly it can induce sufficient pain to prevent him fighting.

Though the outside of the wrist is relatively hard, the inside has many weak spots. Strong, concentrated pressure on these points will make an opponent helpless. Though there are many versions of this technique, only one is dealt with here.

● *Points to Remember*

It is difficult to convey by photographs how pressure is being applied; but in this case *tori* causes intense pain by exerting pressure on the back of *uke's* wrist with the joint at the base of the index finger.

This technique is not effected by a "wringing" action of the arms and nor should it be applied with mere "gripping" power. The student must not be content with executing any technique with the action of the hands only: in the case of *yonkajō osae* it is essential that the power of the hips and the legs should be applied to the opponent's wrist.

By continual practice of *yonkajō* it is possible to develop exceptionally strong and supple hands.

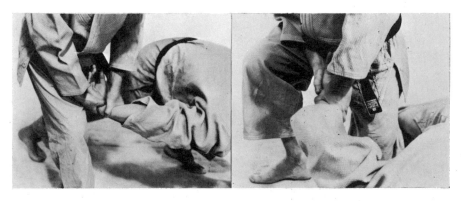

Shōmen-uchi Yonkajō Osae (A)
"Front blow; 4th control"

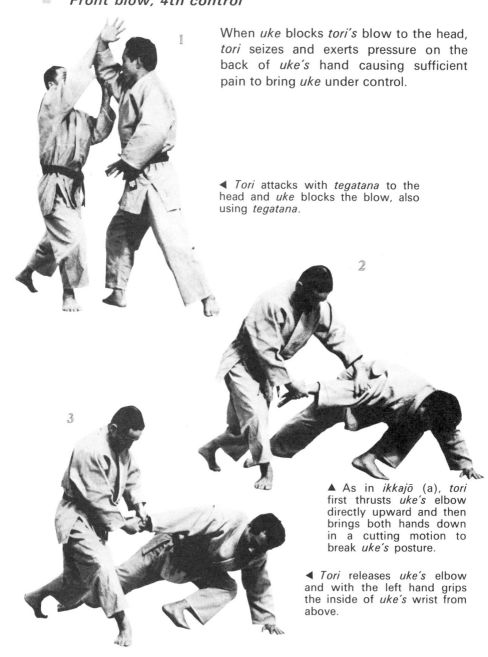

When *uke* blocks *tori's* blow to the head, *tori* seizes and exerts pressure on the back of *uke's* hand causing sufficient pain to bring *uke* under control.

◀ *Tori* attacks with *tegatana* to the head and *uke* blocks the blow, also using *tegatana*.

▲ As in *ikkajō* (a), *tori* first thrusts *uke's* elbow directly upward and then brings both hands down in a cutting motion to break *uke's* posture.

◀ *Tori* releases *uke's* elbow and with the left hand grips the inside of *uke's* wrist from above.

▲ *Tori* advances his left leg to *uke's* right side and, concentrating his strength into the lower joint of his left index finger, strongly applies *yonkajō*.

▶ *Tori* advances his right foot with a big step, goes down onto his left knee and brings *uke* completely under control.

● Finally *uke* changes his grip and holds *uke* with *nikajō*.

SOKUMEN-IRIMI-NAGE
"Side-approach body throw"

WHAT IS SOKUMEN-IRIMI-NAGE?

This technique consists of moving out of the line of *uke's* attack, reinforcing his momentum with one's own force and throwing him from the
side. The use of *irimi* is not limited to this technique: there are instances in
ikkajō and *shihō-nage* where a similar movement is used. *Irimi-nage*,
where *tori* moves into *uke's* side—his weakpoint—to break his posture
and throw him, is a technique peculiar to aikido.

● *Points to Remember*

In the photographs below (*katate-mochi sokumen-irimi-nage* (b)) *tori*
slides his right hand upward across *uke's* neck and face and then sharply
downward in a curving motion; at the same time he takes a pace to *uke's*

rear with his right foot and throws *uke* with a scissor-like movement. Before this stage *tori* has moved out of the line of *uke's* attack and added his own power to *uke's* pushing or pulling movement.

1 Katate-mochi Sokumen-irimi-nage *(A)*
"One hand grasp; side-approach body throw"

When pulled by one hand *tori* utilizes the movement, steps to *uke's* rear and—with a combination of turning the hips, transferring the weight, and hand movement—throws *uke* to the rear.

◀ From *hidari-ai-hanmi*, with his left hand *uke* grasps *tori's* right wrist from the outside and pulls.

● *Tori* immediatley spreads wide the fingers of the hand seized—a reaction typical of all aikido techniques.

▶ Moving with *uke's* pull, *tori* advances his left foot to a point beside the outside of *uke's* left foot and, turning his body and hands about 30° to the left, unbalances *uke*.

4

▲ *Tori* brings his right arm sharply down in a cutting stroke toward his right foot, destroying *uke's* posture and throwing him to the rear.

● Note how well *tori* has preserved his posture. This maintenance of correct attitude (physical and mental) after executing a technique is called *zanshin*. *Zanshin* is most important since it means that *tori* is now in a position to meet a new emergency immediately.

3

◀ At the same time as *tori* makes a big step with his right foot behind *uke*, he thrusts forward and upward with his left hand and delivers *atemi* to *uke's* abdomen with left *te-gatana*.

● If *tori* can bring his right hip into contact with *uke's* left at this point the technique is more effective.

BASIC TECHNIQUES 107

2 Kata-mochi Sokumen-irimi-nage
"Shoulder grasp; side-approach body throw"

When seized from the side at the shoulder and pulled, *tori* moves with the pull, traps *uke's* arm with a downward stroke and, stepping behind *uke*, throws him to the rear.

▲ From *hidari-ai-hanmi*, *uke* grasps *tori's* right shoulder with his left hand (palm downward) and pulls.

▶ *Tori* brings *tegatana* against the outside of *uke's* arm.

▲ Closing the *maai* by stepping forward with the left foot and moving with *uke's* pulling motion, *tori* cuts sharply downward to his left front with right *tegatana* and breaks *uke's* posture.

▶ At the same time *tori* takes a big step with his right foot to *uke's* rear. When *uke* instinctively begins to straighten, *tori* suddenly thrusts upward and "floats" *uke's* weight.

▶ Twisting his hips strongly to the right, *tori* delivers *atemi* with his left hand to *uke's* chest, and cuts down hard with his right hand to his right front, throwing *uke* to his rear.

● *Tori* must keep his eyes on *uke* throughout the whole movement.

SHŌMEN-IRIMI-NAGE
"Front-approach body throw"

WHAT IS SHŌMEN-IRIMI-NAGE?

The *irimi* or body movement differs from that in the previous technique in that *tori* is square to *uke's* side when his body moves in. When *uke* attacks with a striking or stabbing movement, *tori*, synchronizing his movement with *uke's*, pulls him into a whirlpool of motion depriving him of his power and leaving him vulnerable to *tori's* throwing technique.

● *Points to Remember*

If a man is pushed forward his instinctive reaction is to straighten up by pushing backwards. This technique makes subtle use of this movement.

As the photographs show, when *uke* attacks from the front with a blow to the head, *tori* deflects the blow with *tegatana* and breaks *uke's* action, delivers *atemi* to the face with his right hand and then, curving his right arm around *uke's* neck, drives it straight downward while making a big step with his right foot to *uke's* rear. *Uke* is thrown backwards. The important points to remember are to "open" one's body out of the line of attack and to synchronize one's movements with those of *uke's*.

1

Shōmen-uchi Shōmen-irimi-nage
"Front blow; front-approach body throw"

When *uke* attacks from the front with a blow to the head, pivoting on his left foot *tori* makes a 180° turn to the rear breaking *uke's* posture forward and taking advantage of *uke's* reaction, encircles *uke's* neck and face with his right arm and throws him to the rear.

◆ When *uke* attacks from *hidari-gyaku-hanmi* with a blow to the head (*te-gatana*), *tori* "receives" the blow with his right hand, seizes *uke's* collar with his left hand and begins to "lead away" *uke's* arm with his right.

◆ Turning 180° with a big circular motion of his right foot to the rear, *tori* sweeps *uke's* right arm around and downward breaking his posture.

● At the same time *tori's* left hand pushes *uke* forward.

◆ Without resisting *uke's* movement to straighten up, *tori* turns his upper body slightly to the left, moving his weight forward and delivers *atemi* to *uke's* face.

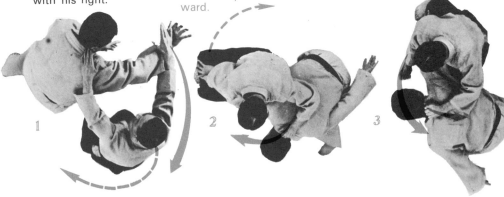

◆ Sliding his right hand around *uke's* neck as though to envelop his face, *tori* "floats" *uke* upward and, as *uke* begins to fall to the rear, *tori* moves his body forward and pushes *uke* strongly down to his (*tori's*) right front.

◆ *Tori* takes a big step with his right foot to *uke's* rear and, with a winding, downward movement of his right arm, throws *uke*.

● In concert with the movement of his right hand, *tori's* left hand holding *uke's* collar pulls strongly downward.
● *Tori's* right hip should be close enough to touch *uke's* right hip.

HIJI-JIME
"Elbow lock"

WHAT IS HIJI-JIME?

Hiji-jime is a technique which bends the joint against its natural movement and is thus a type of *gyaku* (which roughly translated means "lock"). Not all aikido techniques which depend upon the bending of the joints are *gyaku*. *Kime* is the bending of a joint in the direction of its natural movement a little more than normal. *Nikajō* and *sankajō*, which have already been explained, and *kote-gaeshi*, which is explained later, are all *kime*.

● Points to Remember

In *hiji-jime*, *uke's* arm is straightened, his hand gripped firmly, and the pressure on the elbow exerted by the weight of the body. The photographs show *tori* meeting *uke's* attack to the head with *tegatana*, opening his body to the right with a big turn, sweeping *uke's* arm downwards and around, straightening the elbow, trapping the hand and taking a big step to his right front with the right foot, to bring his body weight forward and pressure onto *uke's* elbow.

Mune-mochi Hiji-jime *(B)*
"Chest grasp; elbow lock"

1

When *uke* grips *tori's* lapel and pushes, *tori* opens his body to his right, pivoting on the knee, trapping *uke's* elbow under his left arm.

◀ Both are in *seiza. Uke* grasps *tori's* left lapel with his right hand. *Tori* moves to his left and applies *atemi* with his right hand while his left hand grasps *uke's* right wrist from the outside.

2

▶ Pivoting on the left knee, *tori* turns almost 180° to his right rear, trapping *uke's* elbow under his left arm. *Tori's* left hand presses against the back of *uke's* hand.

● *Uke's* elbow must be held firmly under *tori's* arm.

3

◀ Holding *uke's* wrist with both hands, *tori* turns still more to his right (to bring him 180° from his original position) bringing *uke* forward onto the mat.

4

▶ Advancing his right knee and facing *uke*, *tori* pulls *uke's* arm towards him and presses downwards.

5

● Keep *uke's* wrist into the chest.

KOKYŪ-HŌ
"Breathing method"

WHAT IS KOKYŪ-HŌ?

In everyday Japanese conversation one often hears the words *"kokyū ga au,"* meaning two people are in tune. This quality is essential in practicing aikido: if one is in tune with the opponent it is easier to defeat him, if one is not in tune it is impossible to take advantage of the gaps in his defense. In other words, being in tune with the opponent is the essence of aikido; to attune the spirit is to attune the power.

Kokyū-ryoku ("breathing power") which embodies *shūchū-ryoku*— the ability to concentrate one's power into one particular area of the body—can be generated by regular and diligent practice of certain techniques. One of these is described below; it is called *suwari-ryōte-mochi kokyū-hō*.

● *Points to Remember*

Both are in *seiza*. Synchronizing his movement with *uke's* pull, *tori* raises both hands above his head "floating" *uke*, and brings him to the mat and holds him by "willpower."

This is a method of exercising synchronization, the concentration of strength and, particularly, controlling an opponent using *kokyū-ryoku* and willpower.

As mentioned before *suwari waza* is a fundamental method of developing stability of the hips and if it is practiced regularly the results are reflected in *tachi waza*.

1 Kokyū-hō
"Breathing method"

When *uke* pulls both *tori's* hands, *tori* yields to the pull, pushes forward and upward as if raising a sword and cuts down diagonally to the left, throwing *uke* to his right rear. This is a basic method of learning to channel power along a single, stable line, linking the legs, body and hands.

▲ When both are in *seiza*, *uke* grasps both *tori's* wrists from the outside and pulls. *Tori* reinforces *uke's* movement by thrusting his arms forward and upward as though raising a sword.

● The power behind the pushing movement must run from the feet through the knees, hips, upper body and arms. Furthermore, when pushing, the hips must not "float" far from the heels.

◀ While raising his arms, *tori* comes up onto his toes and, straightening his body, begins to break *uke's* balance to the rear.

◀ Moving his left knee to the left, *tori* cuts down with both arms to his left front.

● Both arms must not be allowed to bend and the cut must be made with *tegatana*.

▶ Pushing and cutting downward with both arms *tori* completely breaks *uke's* balance to the rear.

4

▼ The moment *uke's* back touches the mat *tori* advances his right knee and bears down on *uke*.

5

6

▶ Adjusting his posture (to obtain the most stability) *tori* strives to control *uke* by "willpower."

TENCHI-NAGE
"Heaven and earth throw"

WHAT IS TENCHI-NAGE?

This technique is similar to *ryōte-mochi kokyū-hō* except one hand moves up and the other down, hence, "heaven and earth."

When *uke* seizes both *tori's* wrists and attempts to pull them apart, *tori* yields to the movement and reinforces it with his own power (and *kokyū-ryoku*) to break *uke's* posture and throw him. In the photographs, *tori* raises his right hand above his head in a circular movement, lifting *uke's* left hand from the inside. Using *uke's* right shoulder as the cardinal point, *tori* cuts down with a circular movement of his left hand, taking *uke's* right hand to the rear; at the same time *tori* advances his left knee diagonally to the left. *Uke* is now floated up in a kind of cartwheel and at this moment, *tori* brings his right hand sharply forward and downward in a circular movement and thrusts forward with his left hand to bring *uke* down on his back. *Tori* then advances his right knee to *uke's* side and controls him as in *kokyū-hō* (however, *tori's* hands should be spread a little wider than in *kokyū-hō*).

● *Points to Remember*

The practice of all aikido techniques cultivates *kokyū-ryoku* but *tenchi-nage* is particularly effective in this respect. As its name suggests, the right hand is leading up to the heavens and the left hand is attempting to pierce the earth.

Ryōte-mochi Tenchi-nage
"Both hands held; heaven and earth throw"

Tori pushes one hand upward and the other downward, enveloping *uke* in the movement and throwing him to the rear.

◆ From *hidari-gyaku-hanmi*, *uke* moves forward and grasps both *tori's* wrists. *Tori* steps to his left front with his left foot, pushing down with his left hand and up with his right, lifting *uke's* left hand from the inside.

◆ Transferring his weight to his left foot, *tori* thrusts strongly downward with his left hand and strongly upward in a circular motion with his right hand, breaking *uke's* posture to his right rear.

◆ As soon as *uke's* balance is broken, *tori* takes a big curving step with his right foot to *uke's* rear, bending *uke* further backward.

◆ *Uke's* weight is now "floating" and to throw him with a winding movement, *tori* brings his right arm down in a sweeping, circular motion and thrusts even harder with his left arm to his left front.

● Spread the feet sufficiently and stabilize the body.

◆ *Tori* brings his weight well forward and from that position, with both arms almost encircling *uke*, he thrusts *uke* diagonally to the right, to complete the throw.

KOTE-GAESHI
"Outward wrist twist"

WHAT IS KOTE-GAESHI?

When beginners take up aikido it is often said that it is sufficient if they have enough strength to lift 16 lbs. This is because it is not required that the opponent be picked up and thrown nor that any undue effort be used in bringing the opponent to the ground. The techniques have been devised to exert considerable force with the expenditure of very little strength.

Kote-gaeshi is a very good example. Simply by turning his wrist to the outside, it is possible to break *uke's* posture and bring him to the ground. In other words, by attacking a weak point such as the wrist it is possible to subjugate and control the whole of *uke's* body.

In the photographs, when *uke* seizes *tori's* wrists, *tori* grasps *uke's* right wrist from underneath, releases his left hand and applies left *tegatana*

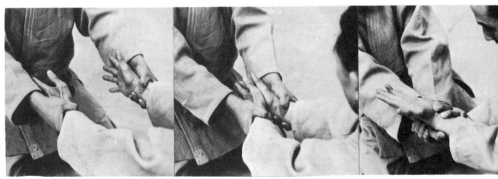

to the back of *uke's* hand, pressing directly downward. This has the effect of throwing *uke*. (If he did not turn over his wrist would break.) *Tori* then grasps *uke's* wrist with his left hand and grips *uke's* elbow bringing him over onto his stomach, by pushing the arm lengthways in the direction of *uke's* face.

● *Points to Remember*

When applying the lock against *uke's* wrist, be sure not to grip with the left hand (if attacking *uke's* right wrist); always use either *tegatana* or the palm of the hand. This is because gripping the wrist limits one's movement: an open hand is freer and can move quickly when necessary. This is one of the essentials of aikido and can be applied to all techniques.

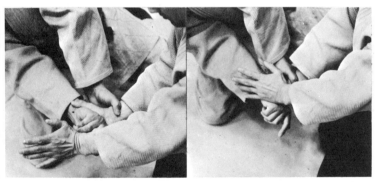

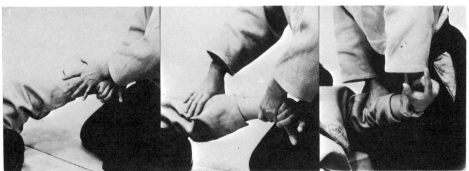

Ryōte-mochi Kote-gaeshi
"Both hands grab; outward wrist twist"

When *uke* has seized both wrists *tori* applies *kote-gaeshi* against one of *uke's* wrists, brings him to the ground and controls him.

▲ From *hidari-ai-hanmi*, *uke* seizes *tori's* wrists. At the same time, *tori* takes back his left foot and brings both his hands together, palm to palm.

▼ Moving against *uke's* right thumb, *tori* releases his left hand, turns *uke's* wrist to his (*uke's*) outside, i.e., away from *tori*, and applies left *tegatana* to the back of *uke's* right hand.

▲ *Tori* turns his left hand palm upwards and simultaneously grasps *uke's* left wrist from below.

▶ While applying strong pressure on *uke's* wrist, *tori* takes a big step forward with his right foot across *uke's* front.

▶ In this position, *tori* turns *uke's* wrist even more and throws him.

● When turning *uke's* wrist, the right hand which is gripping the wrist and the left *tegatana* which is relaxed must move together.

▶ Once *uke* has turned over, while retaining his grip on *uke's* wrist, *tori* moves to his left and changes his grip, grasping the wrist with his left hand and gripping *uke's* elbow with his right. By securing the elbow, he brings *uke* over onto his face.

▶ *Tori* brings *uke* under complete control by pushing *uke's* arm in the direction of his shoulder.

Shōmen-tsuki Kote-gaeshi
"Straight punch; outward wrist twist"

Uke attacks with a stabbing motion from the front; opening his body 90° to the left, *tori* deflects his blow, seizes *uke's* wrist and subdues him with *kote-gaeshi.*

◀ From *hidari-gyaku-hanmi uke* stabs with his right hand at *tori's* abdomen. *Tori*, pivoting on his left foot, takes his right foot back in a 90° turn and with left *tegatana* reinforces the forward movement of *uke's* wrist.

◀ Transferring his weight from the left foot to the right, *tori* turns the upper part of his body 180° (clockwise) and draws *uke's* wrist off to *uke's* right.

▼ *Tori* steps forward with his right foot and throws *uke* by increasing the pressure on his wrist.

▲ As soon as *uke* is unbalanced, *tori* turns back 180° (counter-clockwise), applies *kote-gaeshi* and, opening his right foot to the right, delivers *atemi.*

5

◀ Bringing *uke* onto his face, *to-ri* controls him by pushing the wrists and elbow directly down-ward.

● This is similar to *ryōte-mochi kote-gaeshi* except that the wrist is bent forward.

The preceding sections have dealt with the basic forms of the most frequently used aikido techniques. They are taught in a formalized manner to ensure that after repeated practice all the important elements of the movement will have become reflex actions.

Once this stage has been reached—and not before—the application of the technique to various cases and situations becomes not only possible but a natural reaction. For this reason it is meaningless to dictate what action must be taken if, for instance, you are attacked by a man with a knife. It is doubtful if the expert could explain what he himself would do in any particular situation; his reaction would be instinctive, his technique automatic. However irksome a student may find the repetition of what may often appear to be exaggerated movements, he must accept that this is the only way to achieve the level of skill that may one day save his life. (*Pictured right is kokyū-nage*).

SECTION 4

Practical Application

1 Ikkajō Osae
"1st control"

Here is an example of how *ikkajō* (p. 62) might be adapted. *Tori* grasps *uke's* hand as soon as he feels his wallet being pulled out of his pocket. Obviously he cannot know which technique he is going to use until he realizes what kind of grip he has on *uke's* hand. In this case his training tells him that it is the natural one for *ikkajō*.

Tori turns to face his opponent and finds himself in a familiar situation (fig. 2, *kata-mochi ikkajō osae* (a), p. 68).

In this case there is not enough room nor is it necessary to take *uke* to the ground. Once having broken his balance by pushing his left elbow in the direction of his head, *tori* is able to smash *uke* against the wall.

Note that *tori's* thumb is under *uke's* elbow (4a) and the power of the thrust is coming from *tori's* hips (5).

2 Kote-gaeshi
"Outward wrist twist"

Let us take the same situation as in the previous movement; only this time imagine that *uke* uses his right hand to take the wallet—probably with the idea of making a quick escape to the right of the camera.

Once again *tori* instinctively grasps *uke's* hand but in this instance *tori's* hand naturally falls into the ideal position for applying *kote-gaeshi* (p. 128). *Tori's* pivoting movement to the left will mean that the technique

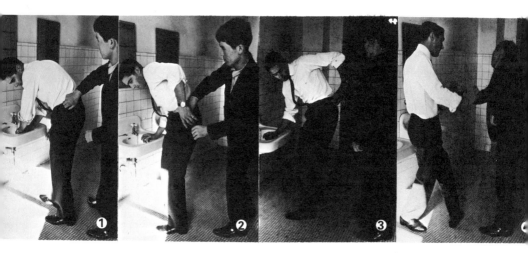

is applied with the whole body not just the local action of the arm; and any attempt by *uke* to continue his movement in the direction of escape will only serve to make the *kote-gaeshi* take effect more quickly.

Once having broken *uke's* balance, *tori* can apply *atemi* to *uke's* exposed jaw (5 and 6); or, by using right *tegatana* against the side of *uke's* neck, simply thrust him into the wall (7).

3

Shihō-nage
"Four-directions throw"

This is almost the textbook version of *shihō-nage* (pp. 48, 49).

Uke has grasped both *tori's* wrists. At the moment he takes hold *tori* extends her fingers (a reaction that should come automatically from continual practice of the basic techniques). *Tori* grasps *uke's* right wrist with her right hand (2). *Tori's* turning movement and the use of her hands and feet are precisely those described on pp. 50, 51.

Note that *tori's* grasping *uke's* wrist and the beginning of her turning movement must be simultaneous.

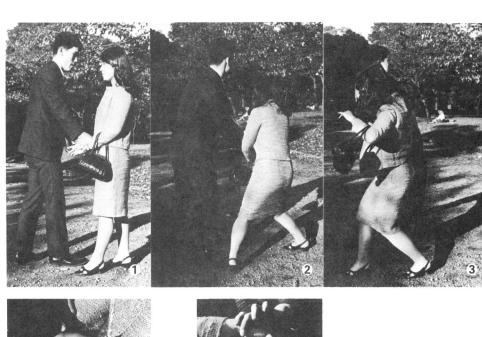

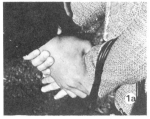

In this situation the assumption is that *uke's* grasping of *tori's* wrists is accompanied by a pushing action which means that *tori* is forced to move back or, as described above, turn away to avoid losing her balance. If there were no attempt to unbalance *tori, uke* would be vulnerable to *atemi* and *shihō-nage* would be neither appropriate nor necessary.

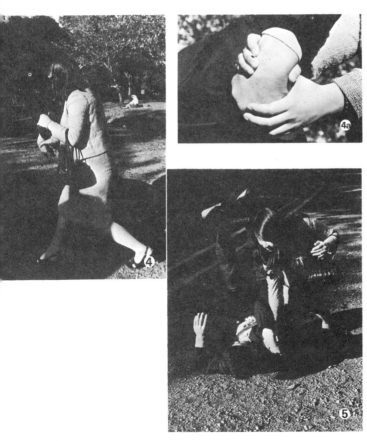

4 Nikajō Osae
"2nd control"

Here is an example of a variation on *nikajō osae*.

Having been grasped around the waist from behind *tori* must first loosen *uke's* grip (2). *Tori* strikes the back of *uke's* hand (roughly in the center) with the second knuckle of the middle finger. The pain will force *uke* to release his grip and the most natural grip *tori* can use to seize *uke's* hand is the one that leads to *nikajō osae*.

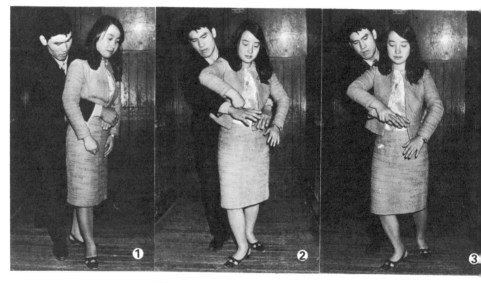

Once *tori* takes a half step forward and turns to face *uke* she is in the same position as fig. 2, p. 76, and from that point onwards the movement is the same as the basic *karate-mochi nikajō osae* (pp. 76, 77) except that as soon as *uke* is brought to his knees *tori* applies *atemi* to the face with her knee since there is no room to complete the basic movement and bring *uke* under complete control.

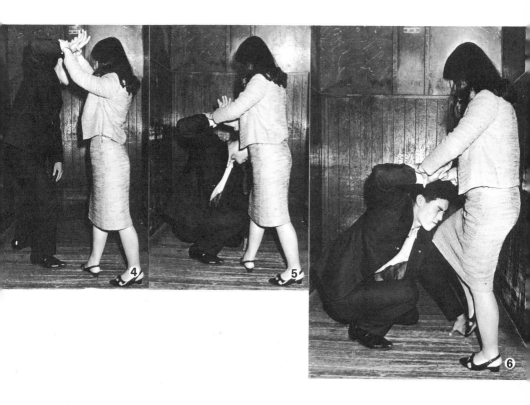

Nikajō Osae
"2nd control"

This is an example where the basic technique can be used without variation—see *kata-mochi nikajō osae* (pp. 84, 85). The great advantage of this technique is that it can be used in confined spaces.

There are two points that must be stressed. It is important to deliver the *atemi* attack the moment *uke* takes hold. The object is not so much to disable him as to momentarily confuse him. During that movement his

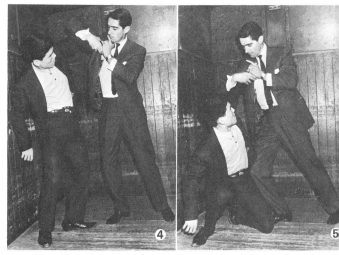

balance must be broken and this is done by the upward glancing movement of *tori's* right *tegatana* (3); so care must be taken not to gloss over this upward movement out of anxiety to begin pushing *uke* to his knees.

Again, unless *uke's* elbow is raised the subsequent downward movement will not be effective.

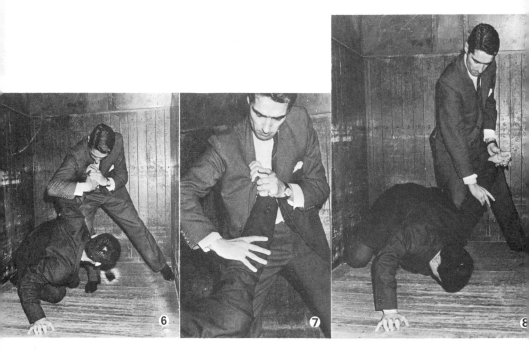

6 Sankajō Osae
"3rd control"

This is a straightforward use of *sankajō*.

Tori breaks *uke's* grip by spreading the elbows and lowering the body (bending the knees, not the waist). As she turns she applys *atemi* to *uke's* solar plexus with elbow and seizes his left hand. It is clear that *tori's* grip is a natural one to use in that position (3) and also happens to be ideal for *sankajō*.

From this point on the movement is orthodox (p. 93), except that once again because of the confined space it is better to smash *uke* into the wall than bring him to the ground and control him.

Note *tori's* feet throughout the movement. She takes half a pace forward with her left foot as she brings *uke's* wrist in front of her (4). While raising the wrist higher she takes another half pace forward with the left foot pivoting on the right foot (5); finally when thrusting *uke* away from her, she steps forward with the right foot (6). Once again, however, it must be pointed out that if the basic techniques have been practiced enough, the foot movement will come naturally.

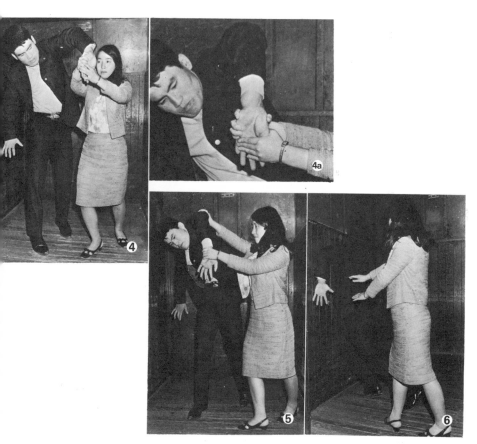

7 Sankajō Osae
"3rd control"

This is another example of *sankajō* (p. 88). The position of *uke's* hand as it comes around *tori's* shoulder offers the perfect opportunity for the grip that leads into *sankajō*. Once having obtained the grip *tori* immediately begins to lower her body (keeping the back straight) and turns (2, 3).

Note the position of *tori's* feet when she secures *uke's* wrist (4). Pictures 4a, b and c show three views of *tori's* hands at that time. *Uke's*

balance is so badly broken at this point that once *tori* shifts her left hand to *uke's* elbow and pushes (5, 5a) it takes little effort to thrust him a considerable distance (6).

Note when twisting *uke's* hand with the left hand (4b) *uke's* hand should be moved in the direction of his armpit.

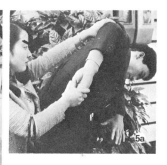
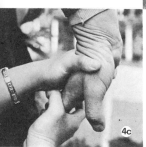

8 Sankajō Osae
"3rd control"

This is almost the basic movement *shōmen-uchi sankajō osae* (pp. 92–94).

The initial movements are the same as in the previous example since *uke's* approach is similar; but once *tori* has reached the position in (4)

the movement is the same as that illustrated from fig. 3 onwards on pages 93 and 94.

In this case, as the incident takes place in an open space, it is possible to go through with the movement and bring *uke* completely under control.

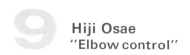

9 Hiji Osae
"Elbow control"

This technique, called *hiji osae*, employs the same principle as *hiji-jime* (pp. 115–117) except that the pressure on *uke's* elbow is applied through the *tegatana*.

Tori senses that *uke* is about to deliver a punch with his right hand and starts to transfer his weight onto his left foot so that he can use it as a pivot and open his body to the right to avoid the attack (1).

Once having seized *uke's* wrist *tori* applies *tegatana* to the elbow and

❶   ❷   ❸

cuts downward in a clockwise, curving movement until *uke's* arm is held firm against *tori's* knee.

This downward sweep must be smooth, synchronized with *uke's* forward movement and it must "whirl" *uke* around *tori's* left leg which is the pivot for *tori's* own turning movement.

Note *tori's* feet must be in the correct position to give him maximum stability throughout the movement.

10 Kokyū Waza
"Breathing techniques"

This is a good example of *kokyū waza* where anticipation, concentration of effort (*shūchū-ryoku*) and synchronization of one's own movement with the opponent's are vital.

Once again *uke* throws a strong punch with his right hand. *Tori* cannot use *hiji osae* as in the previous example because he has the wrong foot forward. Instead, he shifts his weight onto his right foot (1) which he uses as a pivot when turning his hips. At the same time he grasps *uke's* wrist *without stopping its forward movement* (2), synchronizes the anticlockwise turn of his hips with the forward movement of *uke's* body

to reinforce *uke's* (2,3) and thrusts his right arm (cutting edge upward) under *uke's* right arm (3).

By continuing to turn the hips and pulling *uke's* arm downwards in a smooth curving movement to the left he completely destroys *uke's* balance and throws him (4, 5). The "*kokyū*" element in the technique is being able to feel when to exert the concentrated energy i.e., when to start changing the direction of *uke's* forward movement and bring him down in a spiraling motion. Note the *zanshin* (6). *Tori's* posture is still strong and his attention is still on the opponent.

11 Kote-gaeshi
"Outward wrist twist"

This is an example of *kote-gaeshi* being used in a confined and cluttered space—it is not possible for *tori* to use his feet, for example.

As soon as he knows the attack is coming *tori* moves back and places his weight on his left foot which he must use as a pivot to avoid the attack (1). As he opens his body he grips *uke's* hand from above—again not stopping *uke's* forward movement until *uke's* balance is broken (2).

Note carefully the grip (2a) and the position of the thumb (3a).

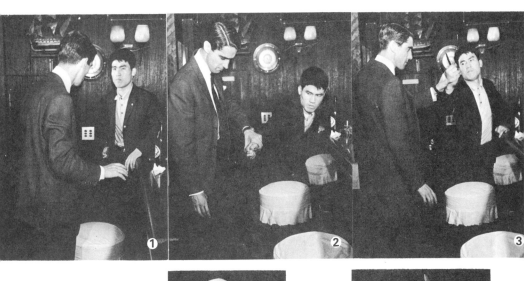

As soon as *uke's* forward movement is spent, *tori* begins to apply *kote-gaeshi*.

It is important that *tori's* right hand should only be applied to, not actually grip *uke's* left hand (4a). A sharp, downward, curving movement of the right hand will bring *uke* to the ground.

Note *tori's* basic stance at the end of the movement (5).

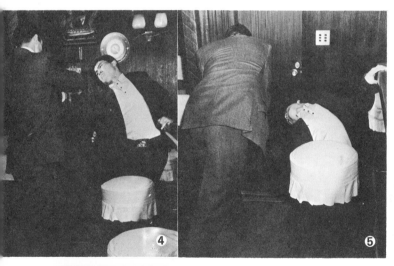

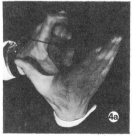

Straight blow

This final movement is a good example of how in some situations simple, short measures can be effective. Indeed, this should be the criterion when considering techniques for self-defense; the less complicated a technique, the faster it can be applied and, more importantly, the less chance there is of failing.

In this situation *uke* has to make a fairly big movement with his right hand after he has picked up the bottle, while *tori* makes a direct movement over a shorter distance.

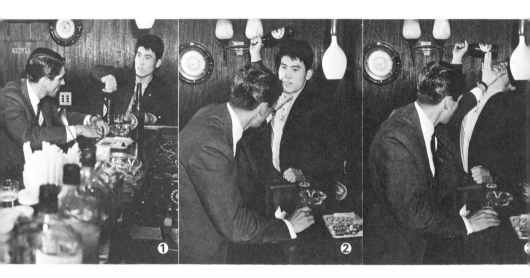

Using the heel of his hand he delivers an upward blow to *uke's* face, at the same time coming to his feet to put the weight of his body into the blow.

Once the blow has been made it is important to maintain contact and, by stepping in with the left foot, push him backwards to the ground.

Glossary

Ai-hanmi: Situation in which opponents face each other in same posture.

Aikidoka: One who participates in aikido.

Atemi: Blows delivered against vulnerable points of the body.

Gyaku-hanmi: Situation in which opponents face each other in different postures.

Hanmi: Standing posture in which one foot is advanced.

Hanmi-hantachi: Situation in which one person is sitting and the other standing.

Hanmi-hantachi waza: Techniques performed when one is sitting and the other standing.

Hidari-hanmi: Left natural posture.

Hiji-jime: Lock applied against the elbow.

Hiji csae: Elbow control.

Hiriki: Elbow power.

Ikkajō osae: 1st control.

Irimi: Literally "putting in the body." *Tori* brings his body into— or almost into—contact with *uke's* body to effect the technique.

Irimi nage: Throw in which *tori* brings his body into contact with, or very close to *uke.*

Kamae: Posture.

Kata: Shoulder.

Katate: One hand.

Kokyū-hō: Literally "breathing method."

Kokyū-ryoku: Breathing power.

Kote-gaeshi: "Outward wrist twist."

Kihon dōsa: Fundamental movement.

Kime: Bending the joint in the direction of natural movement.

Maai: Distance between opponents.
Marui: Circular motion.
Metsubushi: Literally "smashing the eyes."
Migi-hanmi: Right natural posture.
Mochi: Grip.
Mune: Chest.

Nage: Throw.
Nage waza: Throwing technique.
Nikajō osae: 2nd control.

Osae waza: Controlling technique.

Ryoku: Power.
Ryōte: Both hands.

Sankajō osae: 3rd control.
Seiza: Formal sitting position.
Seiza-hō: Moving into formal sitting position.
Shihō-nage: Literally "four directions throw."
Shikkō: Moving on the knees.
Shōmen: Front.
Shūchū: Concentration.
Shūchū-ryoku: Concentration of power.
Shūmatsu dōsa: "Deciding" or "fixing" movement.
Sokumen: Side.
Suri-ashi: Gliding the feet.
Suwari waza: Sitting techniques.

Tachi waza: Standing techniques.

Tegatana: The "cutting" edge of the hand.

Tenchi: Heaven and earth, or up and down.

Tenchi-nage: Heaven and earth throw.

Te waza: Hand techniques.

Tori: The one who applies the technique and the eventual winner.

Tsuki: Thrust.

Uchi: Blow.

Uke: The one who receives the technique and the eventual loser.

Ukemi: Breakfalls.

Waza: Technique.

Yonkajō osae: 4th control.

Yokomen: Side.

Zanshin: Completion of the technique in which awareness of opponent and surroundings is maintained.